= BETTER WAY BOOKS =

SP✸T
&
STAIN
REMOVAL
HANDBOOK

D1319685

Better Way Books has made every effort to ensure the accuracy and reliability of the information, instructions, and directions in this book; however, this is in no way to be construed as a guarantee, and Better Way Books is not liable in case or misinterpretation of the directions, human error, or typographical mistakes.

ISBN 0-88176-319-5

Cover design: Jeff Hapner

CONTENTS

CHAPTER 1
HOW TO MASTER SPOTS & STAINS

It seems that in every household, there's at least one person who leaves behind a trail of stains and spots like a path of gingerbread crumbs: the home handyman who scatters grease spots from garage to attic, the toddler who expresses independence by painting with ball-point pen on the wallpaper; the enthusiastic cook who splatters tomato sauce from ceiling to carpet; the new puppy that pointedly demonstrates its need for house-training. Grass spots on jeans, wine spots on tablecloths, oil stains on the driveway—and what makes it worse is that each stain calls for a different treatment. Catsup on carpet is not treated in the same way as catsup on concrete, and on top of having to identify both the staining agent and the stained surface, you have to work fast. The longer most stains set, the harder they are to remove without damage to the stained surface. If you haven't identified the stain correctly, or if you use an improper stain-removing agent or technique, you may make the stain permanent and cause additional damage to the stained object.

THREE TYPES OF STAINS ON FABRICS

Generally, stains can be divided into three types. Each type dictates certain general treatment procedures.

Greasy Stains. Lubricating and cooking oils, butter, machine grease, and similar substances produce greasy stains. Grease spots are sometimes removed from washable fabrics by hand or machine laundering. Pretreating by rubbing a little detergent directly into the spot often helps, as does using a dry-cleaning solvent on the stain. If you are treating an old stain or one that has been ironed, a yellow stain may remain after treatment with a solvent. Bleach is often effective at eliminating this yellow residue.

To remove grease spots from nonwashable fabrics, sponge the stain from center to edge with dry-cleaning solvent. Removal may take several applications, and the spot should be allowed to dry completely before each sponging. Greasy stains may also be removed from nonwashable fabrics by using an absorbent substance such as cornstarch, cornmeal, French chalk, or fuller's earth. Absorbents are dusted on greasy spots to pick up the grease. When the absorbent material begins to look caked, it should be shaken or brushed off. Repeat this procedure until most of the stain is gone.

Absorbents are easy to use and will not harm fabrics. However, the other stain removal agents (detergent, dry-cleaning solvent, and bleach) can damage fibers; before using them you should carefully read the care label on the stained item and the label on the product container.

Nongreasy Stains. Nongreasy stains are produced by materials such as tea, coffee, fruit juice, food coloring, and ink. If you have such a stain on a washable fabric, the best treatment is to sponge the stain with cool water as soon as possible. If this doesn't work, try soaking the fabric in cool water. The stain may soak out within half an hour, or you may need to leave the item in the water overnight. If some stain still remains, gently rub liquid detergent into it and rinse with cool water. The last resort is to use bleach, but read the fabric care label first. If the stain is old or has been ironed, it may be impossible to remove it completely.

A nongreasy stain on a nonwashable fabric can also be sponged with cool water. Or, you can place a disposable diaper or other absorbent pad beneath the stained area and slowly and carefully flush the stain by pouring water onto it using a mister or eyedropper. You must control the amount of water and the rate at which it is poured to avoid spreading the stain. This may be sufficient to remove some stains, especially if treatment is started promptly. If not, work liquid detergent into the stain as described above and rinse by flushing or sponging with cool water. Sponge the stain with rubbing alcohol after rinsing to remove detergent residue and to speed drying. (**Caution:** If treating acetate, acrylic, modacrylic, rayon, triacetate, or vinyl, dilute 1 part alcohol with 2 parts water.)

Combination Stains. Coffee with cream, Thousand Island salad dressing, and lipstick are items that cause combination stains; that is, they combine greasy and nongreasy elements. Such stains may require double treatment—first the nongreasy elements of the stain should be treated, then the greasy residue should be removed. The first step in treating such stains is to sponge with cool water as described above, then work liquid detergent into the stain and rinse thoroughly. After the fabric has dried, apply dry-cleaning fluid to any remaining greasy portion of the stain with a sponge. Allow the fabric to dry. Repeat applications of cleaning fluid if necessary.

THE GROUND RULES

The following rules apply to almost every spot and stain. Rules number one and two are cardinal in treating every spot and stain.

1. The quicker, the better. The best time to treat a stain is within moments of its occurrence. The longer a stain sets, the more likely it is to become permanent.

2. Identify or try to identify both the staining agent and the stained surface before you begin treatment. Both factors affect how you treat the stain. Cotton is treated differently from rayon or silk. Knowing what the stained surface is helps you choose the proper treatment technique and avoid damaging the surface.

3. Remove as much as possible of the staining agent before treatment with a stain-removal product. Be careful not to spread the stain when removing the excess staining material.

4. Handle stained items gently. Rubbing, folding, wringing, or squeezing can cause the stain to penetrate more deeply and may damage delicate fibers.

5. Avoid using heat. Don't use hot water on stains, don't dry stained articles with heat, and never iron stained fabrics. Heat can make a stain impossible to remove.

6. Pretest any stain-removing agent. Even water may damage some surfaces, so always run a sample test on some inconspicuous spot.

7. Follow directions to the letter. Read all the manufacturer's directions on the product container. If you make your own cleaning supplies, be sure you're using the proper ingredients and that you are using the cleaning agent exactly as described.

8. Work from the center of the stain outward. Most stains are best treated with movements that are directed outward. Such movements help avoid leaving a ring around the cleaned area.

CHAPTER 2
UNDERSTANDING FABRIC CARE LABELS

Permanently attached care labels have been required on almost all garments manufactured or sold in the United States since 1972. Care labels are also required on garments made of suede and leather, upholstered furniture, draperies, most bed linens, tablecloths, towels, and slipcovers. Fabric stores must supply care labels whenever a consumer purchases fabric other than remnants less than 10 yards long. These labels can be of enormous help in determining exactly how you should go about removing stains, because, in addition to giving care instructions, they identify fiber content. This is especially important in light of the widespread use of blends in modern garments. When removing spots and stains, *you should follow procedures recommended for the most delicate fiber in the blend.* To remove stains from a blend of cotton and silk, use the procedure recommended for silk. If after such treatment, the stain is still apparent, follow the procedure for cotton, the more durable fiber in this blend.

MACHINE WASHABLE

When label reads:	It means:
Machine wash	Wash by any customary method, including commercial laundering (If no bleach statement is made, then all types of bleach may be used)
Do not commercially launder	Use laundering methods designed for residential use or use in a self-service establishment
Warm wash Warm rinse	Use warm water or warm washing machine setting 90°F to 110°F (hand comfortable)
Cold wash Cold rinse	Use cold water from tap or cold washing machine setting (temperature up to 85°F)
Bleach when needed	All bleaches may be used when necessary
No bleach	No bleaches may be used
Only non-chlorine bleach when needed	Chlorine bleach may not be used
Wash separately	Wash alone or with like colors

MACHINE WASHABLE

When label reads:	It means:
Delicate or gentle cycle	Use appropriate machine setting (slow agitation and reduced time)
Durable press cycle Permanent press	Use appropriate machine setting (cool down or cold rinse before short spin cycle)
No spin	Remove wash load before final machine spin cycle

NONMACHINE WASHING

When label reads:	It means:
Hand wash	Launder only by hand at hand comfortable water temperature (If no bleach statement made all bleaches may be used)
Hand wash with like colors	Launder only by hand with colors of similar hue and intensity.

HOME DRYING

When label reads:	It means:
Tumble dry	Dry in tumble dryer at specified setting—high, medium, low or no heat

HOME DRYING

When label reads:	It means:
Tumble dry Remove promptly	Same as above, but in absence of cool down cycle remove at once when tumbling stops
Drip dry	Hang wet and allow to dry with hand shaping only
Line dry	Hang damp and allow to dry
No wring No twist	Hang dry, drip dry or dry flat only; handle to prevent wrinkles and distortion
Dry flat	Lay garment on flat surface
Block to dry	Maintain original size and shape while drying

IRONING OR PRESSING

When label reads:	It means:
Cool iron	Set iron at lowest setting
Warm iron	Set iron at medium setting
Hot iron	Set iron at hot setting
Do not iron	Do not iron or press with heat

IRONING OR PRESSING

When label reads:	It means:
Steam iron	Iron or press with steam
Iron damp	Dampen garment before ironing

MISCELLANEOUS

When label reads:	It means:
Dry clean	May be dry cleaned by normal method or in coin-operated dry cleaning machine
Professionally dry clean	Included with this term will be other instructions to be followed by your professional dry cleaner

Reprinted with permission of the Consumer Affairs Committee, American Apparel Manufacturers Association

CHAPTER 3
WHAT TO HAVE ON HAND

In order to treat stains and spots as soon as they occur, you have to be prepared. You should always have on hand the cleaning supplies and household products appropriate for treating the stains likely to occur in your home. This chapter lists stain-removing agents by category. It tells you where to purchase these supplies and for what they are used. Because many of these products are flammable or toxic, certain safety tips should be kept in mind when storing and using them.

- Store stain-removing products carefully, out of the reach of children. The storage area should be cool, dry, and apart from food storage areas. Keep bottles tightly capped, boxes closed.
- Do not transfer cleaning products to new containers. Keep them in their original containers so that you never have to search for directions for their proper use and so that they are always clearly labeled.
- Follow the directions on the product label and heed all warnings.
- Glass or unchipped porcelain containers are preferable to metal or plastic when working with stain-removal agents. Never use plastic with solvents. Never use any container that is rusty. Clean all containers thoroughly after use.

- Protect your hands with rubber gloves and don't touch your eyes or skin while handling stain-removal chemicals. If you do accidentally touch your eyes, or spill chemicals on your skin, flush immediately with clear water.
- Remember that the fumes of solvents are toxic; work in a well-ventilated area.
- Do not use chemicals near an open flame or electrical outlet. Do not smoke while using chemicals.
- Do not use a solvent as a laundry additive.
- When using a solvent on a washable fabric, be sure to rinse all traces of the solvent out of the fabric.
- Don't experiment with mixtures of stain-removal agents. Never combine products unless specifically directed to do so. (See Chapter 5.) Such combinations can be dangerous.
- If the cleaning process requires the use of more than one stain-removal agent, rinse each out before applying the next. In addition to the solvents, bleaches, detergents, and chemicals you'll probably need, there are certain items you should have ready for a spot or stain catastrophe. The following are the basic tools used in treating most stains:

> Clean white cotton cloths
> Disposable diapers, white blotting paper or towels
> Spoon, blunt knife, or spatula
> Eyedropper, trigger spray bottle, or mister (the kind used for misting houseplants)
> Small brush
> Several colorfast weights

STAIN-REMOVAL AGENTS

Check through the listing of stains in Chapter 5 for the stains that occur most frequently in your household. Read the treatment to find which of the following stain-removing agents you're most likely to need. Most are available at grocery stores, hardware stores, or pharmacies.

ABSORBENTS

Substances used as absorbents "soak up" stains, epecially grease stains. Materials used as absorbents include cornstarch, cornmeal (usually considered the best for lighter colors), white talcum powder, or fuller's earth (best for use on darker colors, available at pharmacies and garden supply stores). Absorbents are used on light or new stains; they will damage neither fabrics nor other surfaces and they are easy to use. The absorbent material is spread on the stained area and allowed to work. As the grease is soaked up, the absorbent material will cake or become gummy. It should then be shaken or brushed off. The process should be repeated until most of the stain has been removed. Some light stains may be completely removed if the absorbent is left on for 8 hours or more.

BLEACHES

Chlorine. Commonly used to bleach white cotton, linen, and synthetic fabrics, chlorine bleach can also be used as a disinfectant and stain remover. Chlorine bleach is potent and can weaken fibers. If allowed to soak in a bleach solution too long, even cotton and linen will be weakened. Chlorine bleach should not be used on silk, wool, or fabrics exposed to sunlight (curtains, for example). To avoid damaging your fabric, always pretest bleach on a hidden area and rinse all bleached items thoroughly. **Caution:** Chlorine bleach is poisonous. If it comes in contact with the skin or eyes, it will cause burns and irritation. Read all warnings on the label.

Color Remover. Color removers contain hydrosulfite chemicals and are used both for stain removal and to lighten the color of fabrics before they are redyed a lighter color. They are safe for colorfast fibers, but they fade or remove many dyes. Always pretest color removers on an inconspicuous corner of the article you are treating. If the product causes a distinct color change rather than fading, rinse with water immediately and you may be able to restore the original color. However, if the colors fade when the color remover is applied, the original color cannot be restored. Color remover should not be used or stored in metal containers. **Rit Color Remover** (Special Products, an Affiliate of CPC North America) is a good product and can be found in drug, grocery, and variety stores. **Caution:** Color removers are poisonous. Avoid prolonged contact with skin. Observe all precautions on the label.

Hydrogen Peroxide. The 3% solution of hydrogen peroxide sold in drugstores as a mild antiseptic is a good bleach, safe for most surfaces and all fibers (though dyed fabrics should be pretested for colorfastness). Be careful not to purchase the stronger solution sold for bleaching hair. Peroxide should be stored in a cool dark place. Buy small quantities; it loses strength if stored for a long time. Do not use or store peroxide in metal containers. If you pour out too much peroxide, do not pour the excess back in the bottle as peroxide is easily contaminated.

Sodium Perborate. You can purchase sodium perborate under trade names or generically at drugstores. Sold in crystal form, sodium perborate is safe for all fabrics and surfaces, although, once again, pretesting is recommended to assure that your fabric is colorfast. This oxygen-type bleach is slower-acting than hydrogen peroxide. When using this bleach, be sure to rinse treated articles thoroughly.

CHEMICALS

Acetic Acid. A 10% solution of acetic acid can be purchased generically at pharmacies. (White vinegar is 5% acetic acid and can be used as a substitute for the stronger solution.) It is a clear fluid that can be used to remove stains on silk and wool. It must be diluted with 2 parts water for use on cotton and linen (a pretest is recommended). It should not be used on acetate. If acetic acid causes a color change, sponge the affected area with ammonia.

Acetone. Acetone can be purchased generically at pharmacies and hobby shops. A colorless liquid that smells like peppermint, it can be used on stains caused by substances such as fingernail polish or household cement. Although it will not damage either natural fibers or most synthetics, it should be pretested to make sure that dyed fabrics will not be harmed. It should not be used on fabrics containing acetate. Use only pure acetone on stains; although most nail polish removers contain acetone, the other ingredients included in these products can worsen stains. **Caution:** Acetone is flammable and evaporates rapidly, producing toxic fumes. When using acetone, work outside or in a well-ventilated place. Avoid inhaling fumes. Store in a tightly capped container in a cool place.

Alcohol. Common isopropyl alcohol (70%), which can be purchased generically at drugstores, is sufficient for most stain-removal jobs that call for alcohol, although the stronger denatured alcohol (90%) can also be used. Be sure you don't buy alcohol with added color or fragrance. Alcohol will fade some dyes; pretest before using it. Alcohol will damage acetate, tri-acetate, modacrylic, and acrylic fibers. If you must use it on fibers in the acetate family, dilute the alcohol with two parts water. **Caution:** Alcohol is poisonous and flammable. Observe all label precautions.

Ammonia. For stain removal, purchase plain household ammonia without added color or fragrance. It is sold at grocery stores. Because ammonia affects some dyes, always pretest on a hidden corner of the stained article. To restore color changed by ammonia, rinse the affected area with water and apply a few drops of white vinegar. Rinse with clear water again. Ammonia damages silk and wool; if you must use it on these fibers, dilute it with an equal amount of water and use as sparingly as possible. **Caution:** Ammonia is poisonous. Avoid inhaling its fumes. It will cause burns or irritation if it comes in contact with the skin or eyes. Observe all label precautions.

Amyl Acetate. Buy chemically pure amyl acetate (banana oil) for use in stain removal. It is available at drugstores. It is safe for use on fibers that could be damaged by acetone, but it should not be allowed to come in contact with plastics or furniture finishes. **Caution:** Amyl acetate is poisonous and flammable. Avoid contact with the skin and inhaling the vapors.

Coconut Oil. Coconut oil is sold in drug and health food stores. It is used in the preparation of a Dry Spotter (see How to Make Dry and Wet Spotters in this chapter), which is used to remove many kinds of stains. If you cannot obtain coconut oil, you may substitute mineral oil which is almost as effective.

Glycerine. Glycerine is sold generically in pharmacies. It is used in the preparation of the Wet Spotter (see How to Make Dry and Wet Spotters in this chapter), which is used to remove many kinds of stains.

Oxalic Acid. Effective in treating ink and rust stains, oxalic acid crystals are sold in many pharmacies. Before using them, you must dissolve the crystals in water (1 tablespoon crystals to 1 cup warm water). Pretest the solution on a hidden corner before using it on the stain. Moisten the stained area with the solution. Allow to dry, then reapply, keeping the area moist until the stain is removed. Be sure all traces of the solution are rinsed out. **Caution:**

Oxalic acid is poisonous. Avoid all contact with the skin and eyes and wear rubber gloves.

Sodium Thiosulfate. Available in crystal form at drugstores and photo supply houses, sodium thiosulfate is also known as photographic "hypo" or fixer. Although considered safe for all fibers and harmless to dyes, it should be tested on an inconspicuous area of fabric before use. **Caution:** Observe all label precautions.

Turpentine. Turpentine is commonly found in paint and hardware stores and in art supply houses. Most often used as a thinner for oil-base paints, it is effective on paint and grease stains, but it must be used carefully. **Caution:** Turpentine is flammable and poisonous. Observe all label precautions.

Vinegar. Only white vinegar should be used for stain removal. Cider and wine vinegar have color that can leave a stain. Vinegar can be purchased at grocery stores and pharmacies. It contains a 5% acetic acid solution and should be diluted if you must use it on cotton or linen. Vinegar is safe for all other colorfast fibers, but can change the color of some dyes, so always test its effects on an inconspicuous area first. If a dye changes color, rinse the affected area with water and add a few drops of ammonia. Rinse thoroughly with water again.

DRY-CLEANING SOLVENTS

Perchloroethylene, trichloroethane, and trichloroethylene are three of the most common and effective ingredients in the dry-cleaning solvents found on the market today. Most of these solvents are nonflammable, but their fumes are toxic and should not be inhaled. Not all spot removers/dry-cleaning solvents can be used on all surfaces, nor will all products remove all stains, so be sure to read the labels before using. Dry-cleaning solvents are available at pharmacy, grocery, variety, and hardware stores. A few exceptional products are **Carbona No. 10 Special Spot Remover, Carbona Cleaning Fluid,** and **Carbona Spray Spot Remover** (Carbona Products Company), **K2r Spot-lifter** (Texize) (tube and aerosol forms) **Brush Top Spot Remover** (Scot Laboratories Division of Scott & Fetzer), **Afta Cleaning Fluid** and **Afta Spot Wipes** (Afta Solvents Corporation), and **Amway Remove Fabric Spot Cleaner** (Amway Corp.).

Note: Carbona No. 10 Special Spot Remover and Carbona Cleaning Fluid are chemically identical. Carbona No. 10 Special Spot Remover is sold in a bottle with a built-in fabric applicator top, while the cleaning fluid is packaged in a can. The former is more convenient to use for many spots, but the cleaning fluid usually is substantially cheaper and can be applied with a sponge or absorbent pad.

SHAMPOOS AND STAIN REMOVERS
FOR CARPETS

To use a foam carpet shampoo, simply spray it on, rub or sponge it in if instructions require it, then vacuum when dry. Follow the manufacturer's directions and always pretest in an inconspicuous corner to be certain the fiber is colorfast. You may have to shampoo the entire carpet if removing the spot leaves a brighter patch. Some very good carpet shampoos are **Carbona 1 Hour Rug Cleaner** (Carbona Products Company), **Glory Professional Strength Rug Cleaner** (S.C. Johnson & Son, Inc.), and **Lestoil Deodorizing Rug Shampoo** (Noxell Corporation).

To remove small spots, apply a carpet stain-removing product such as **Afta Carpet Stain Remover** (Afta Solvents Corporation), **Spot Shot Carpet Stain Remover** (Sifers Chemicals, Inc.), **Stain-X Carpet Stain Remover** (Positive Products Laboratories, Inc.) or **Up & Out** (Trewax Company). Up & Out is not for use on wool carpets.

SPECIALTY PRODUCTS

Leather and Vinyl Conditioners. **The Tannery** (Missouri Hickory Corp.) can remove many stains from leather and vinyl, while conditioning the surface at the same time. It is easy to use and in many cases restores the luster and suppleness on poorly maintained leathers. Be sure to read the label carefully. **Fiebing's Saddle Soap** (Fiebing Company, Inc.) and **Vinyl Magic** (Magic American Chemical Corp.) also are good leather and vinyl cleaners/conditioners.

Mildew Removers. **X-14 Instant Mildew Stain Remover** (White Laboratories, Inc.) is a very good mildew remover for most surfaces. It is not recommended for fabrics. It kills the mildew spores on contact and prevents restaining. Be sure to read the label carefully. Using **Afta Mildew Stop** (Afta Solvents Corporation), available in aerosol and dry packet forms, is a good preventive measure for mildew-prone areas.

Rust Removers. **Bar Keepers Friend Cleanser & Polish** (SerVaas Laboratories, Inc.) is an abrasive that works very well on rust stains. It is safe for most fabrics, though be sure to read the label. It will also remove tarnish, coffee and tea stains, fruit and vegetable stains, and smoke. **Pumice Scouring Stick** (United States Pumice Company) and **Whink Rust Stain Remover** (Whink Products Company) also are effective.

Suede Cleaners. **Suede Stone** (Canden Company) is a product for rubbing marks from suede. Usually, rubbing is all that is needed to remove grime, dirt, and oil stains; however, it can be dampened for tougher stains. It will also remove some types of marks from wallpaper, much like an eraser. Be sure to read label directions and restrictions carefully. **Child Life Suede & Fabric Cleaner** is an excellent all-around cleaner and conditioner.

Tile and Grout Cleaners. For removing stains from grout without chipping, use **Afta Tile & Grout Cleaner** (Afta Solvents Corporation), baking soda, or powdered cleanser. For mildew stains, apply **Carbona Tile and Bath Cleaner** (Carbona Products Company) to the grout and ceramic tile to kill all mildew.

Wallpaper Cleaner. Crayon marks and graphite can be removed from wallpaper, woodwork, linoleum, marble, and brick with **Crayerase** (Canden Company), a nontoxic cleaning bar.

WASHING AGENTS

Detergents. When stain-removal directions call for mild detergent, choose a white dishwashing liquid detergent; the dyes in nonwhite detergents may worsen your stain. If instructions call for a pretreating paste made of detergent and water, use a powdered detergent that does not contain bleach. If the stain-removal directions specify that you should apply a liquid laundry detergent directly to the spot or stain, be sure to read label directions carefully. Some products cannot safely be used in this manner. Other detergent products (those used in automatic dishwashers or for heavy household cleaning, and certain laundry products) may contain alkalies that could set stains.

Enzyme Presoaks. Most effective on protein stains (meat juices, eggs, blood, and the like), enzyme presoaks may harm silk and wool. Make sure you've exhausted every alternative before you use enzyme presoaks on these two fabrics. Use as soon as possible after mixing in solution; enzyme presoak solutions become inactive in storage. Two very good enzyme products are **Axion** (Colgate-Palmolive Company) and **Biz** (Procter & Gamble). Be sure to read and observe all label directions.

Powdered Cleansers. Scouring powders and baking soda can be used to remove stains on surfaces that won't be harmed by abrasives. However, you should be aware that prolonged or overly vigorous scrubbing with these products can scratch the most durable surface. Make sure you rinse away all of the powder when the job is completed.

Pretreaters. Pretreaters are used on spots and stains that might not respond to normal laundering procedures. They start the cleaning process before the stained item is put in the washer. Pretreaters must be used in conjunction with the rest of the laundering process; do not try to use them alone as though they were spot removers. After applying a pretreater, do not allow the fabric to dry before washing. Follow label directions. Some good brands are **Shout Laundry Soil & Stain Remover** (S.C. Johnson & Son, Inc.), **Spray 'n Wash** (Textile), **Magic Pre-Wash** (Armour-Dial Inc.), and **Miracle White Laundry Soil & Stain Remover** (The Drackett Company).

Soaps. Do not use bath soaps with added moisturizers, fragrance, dyes, or deodorant to treat spots and stains. Purchase either laundry soap or pure white soap.

HOW TO MAKE DRY AND WET SPOTTERS

To mix a Dry Spotter, combine 1 part coconut oil (available at pharmacies and health food stores) and 8 parts liquid dry-cleaning solvent. This solution may be stored if the container is tightly capped to prevent evaporation of the solvent. Mineral oil may be substituted for the coconut oil, but is not quite as effective. **Caution:** Dry-cleaning solvents are poisonous and may be flammable. Follow all of the precautions given under Dry-cleaning Solvents.

To prepare a Wet Spotter, mix 1 part glycerine, 1 part white dishwashing detergent, and 8 parts water. Shake well before each use. Store Wet Spotter in a plastic squeeze bottle.

CHAPTER 4
SPECIAL TECHNIQUES

Basically, there are two approaches to removing spots and stains. You can use a stain-removal agent (see Chapter 3) that interacts with the stain chemically, or you can physically loosen or remove the stain from the surface. Many stubborn stains require both chemical and physical treatment. In this chapter, we discuss eight physical stain-removal techniques: brushing, flushing, freezing, presoaking, pretreating, scraping, sponging, and tamping.

BRUSHING

Brushing is used to remove dried stains and spots. Some spots, such as those formed of dried mud, may be completely removed by brushing. In treating other types of dry stains (for example, face powder), brushing is just the first step in treating the stain. In treating some stains, brushing may be one of the last steps, as when you want to remove an absorbent or a dried stain-removing paste from a surface.

Use a small, stiff-bristled brush for this technique. A toothbrush works well on small stains. When working on a fabric, stretch the piece on a firm, clean working surface. Hold a clean sheet of paper next to the stain (on walls, hold the paper beneath the stain) so that you can brush the staining material onto the paper.

Use a gentle motion to brush the stain up off the surface and onto the paper. It may help to blow softly on the spot as you brush.

FLUSHING

Flushing is used to remove loosened staining materials and any residue from the stain-removal agent. This is an important step in the process, for if any chemicals are left in the material, they may cause additional staining or they may damage the treated article.

When flushing a stain, especially one on a nonwashable fabric, you need to control the flow of water carefully. To apply a measured amount of flushing liquid, use a device such as an eyedropper or plant mister, or a plastic trigger spray bottle that can be adjusted to spray a fine stream. Before you begin the treatment, place a clean absorbent pad beneath the spot, then slowly and carefully apply the recommended stain remover to the stain. If you decide to use a mister, place the tip against the stained area and depress the plunger or pump the trigger slowly. In this way, you can force out a thin stream of fluid without wetting a large area. You must work slowly; do not apply the liquid faster than the pad beneath can absorb it and do not spread the stain. Replace the absorbent pad frequently so that the deposited staining material does not restain the fabric.

Stains on area rugs may be flushed following the directions above. In fact, any rug under which you can place an absorbent pad can be treated by flushing. If, however, your rug is too large to lift or if the stain is on tacked-down rugs or carpeting, you may have to sponge the stain-removal agent onto the spot instead. Then sponge with clear water to remove chemical residues. Remember, the pad or cloth used for sponging must be changed frequently.

If you are treating a washable fabric and directions call for flushing with water, you may rinse the stained article. To rinse out a stain, dip the article up and down repeatedly in a container of warm water. Change the rinse water frequently.

PRETREATING

Pretreating is used to ease the removal of small stains, especially those that are oily or greasy. Stubborn soil, such as the ground-in dirt on collars, cuffs, and socks, is easier to remove after it's been pretreated. When you are pretreating a stain, you apply the stain-removing agent directly to the stained area. To pretreat a stain, you may use a liquid detergent, a soil-and-stain-removing pretreat spray, bar soap, or a pretreating paste made of powdered detergent (do not use one that contains bleach) and water.

Liquid detergent and pretreating sprays should be applied directly onto the dry stain. If you are using bar soap or have prepared a paste of powdered or granular detergent and water, dampen the fabric slightly before applying the pretreating agent. After its application, rub the pretreater into the stain gently, then wash the item as you normally do.

To use pretreating sprays successfully, you should keep a few points in mind. Pretest the spray by applying it to an inconspicuous part of the garment before using it on the stain. Most of these sprays are perfectly safe on all washable fabrics, but some contain an oxygen-type bleach ingredient that could harm some dyes. Apply the product according to package directions, wait 5 minutes, and then rinse the pretest area carefully. If no color change is apparent, you can safely treat the stain. After using one of these sprays, it is essential that you wash the treated article thoroughly to remove both the rest of the stain and any residue from the pretreat spray. Allowing the residue to set may cause a new stain.

PRESOAKING

Presoaking is a useful and effective treatment for washable articles that are grayed, yellowed, or heavily stained. You can presoak laundry in the washer or in a sink or tub. Use warm water. Sort the soiled items before presoaking; noncolorfast items should be soaked separately or with similar colors and for only a short time.

How long you should presoak stained articles depends upon the stain and the fiber. For most stains, 30 minutes should be adequate. Noncolorfast items should be soaked only briefly. Heavily stained items or stains that have set for a long time may require overnight soaking.

You may want to add bleach, laundry detergent, or an enzyme presoak product to the soaking water. However, avoid using enzyme products on silk or wool, and do not use chlorine bleach and an enzyme product at the same time. Whenever you add anything to the water used for presoaking, make sure that the item is then thoroughly rinsed before you launder it. There should not be any residue from the presoak product left in the item when it is washed.

SCRAPING

Scraping can be used to lift off excess semisolid staining material and to loosen caked-on stains. Removal of as much of such materials as possible makes it easier for the stain-removing agent to reach the surface, and although scraping may not remove a stain completely, it is often a necessary step before applying a stain remover.

Do not use an absorbent pad beneath an item you are going to scrape. For your scraping tool use a dull knife, spoon, or spatula. Don't press hard, but move the edge of your scraping tool back and forth across the stain in short strokes. Be gentle to avoid damaging the stained surface. To remove some stains you must add liquid as you scrape, working the liquid into the stain as you remove excess material.

FREEZING

Some staining substances, such as candle wax and gum, can be hardened by the application of cold so that they are easier to remove. Work fast when treating a spill that is still semisolid. You may be able to limit the area stained by quickly hardening the staining material. To freeze a stain, hold one or more ice cubes against it. If the stained item is not washable, place the ice in a plastic bag. If the stained item is portable and the stain is large, you may put the article into a plastic bag and place it in the freezer. Take the item out when the staining material solidifies.

After the stain has solidified, it can usually be gently lifted or scraped from the surface. Any residue may require further stain-removal treatment.

SPONGING

Sponging is one of the most frequently used methods of applying many stain-removing agents, including water. Sponging is another technique in which clean absorbent pads are used. The stained item should be laid on a pad, stainside down, if possible. You may have to sponge stains on carpets without any absorbent pad beneath it, in which case you must be especially careful to wet the carpet as little as possible.

Use another clean pad or a clean sponge to apply the stain-removing agent. Dampen this pad with the agent specified in the stain-removal directions and sponge the stain gently. Use light strokes and work outward from the center of the stain. Try to keep your sponging strokes as close to the stain as possible. Use only enough stain remover to dampen the sponge and move in an irregular pattern. By following these directions, you are less likely to cause rings to form.

Check the pad beneath the stain at frequent intervals and examine the sponging pad as well. Change the pad as soon as any stain is deposited on it. In this way, the staining agent will not be reapplied to the fabric.

Certain fabrics, including acetate, triacetate, and rayon, are more likely than others to develop rings when treated with this technique. So, when sponging stains on these fabrics, you must be even more careful. Barely wet the sponge with stain remover and touch the fabric lightly so that the stain remover is absorbed as slowly as possible. Limit your strokes to the immediate stained area to keep the moistened area as small as possible and avoid spreading the stain. After the stain is removed, dry the fabric as quickly as possible. Blot the treated area gently between clean, dry absorbent pads; then allow it to dry. Unless you have used only water as the stain-removal agent, do not use heat in drying.

TAMPING

Tamping is a stain-removal technique that is effective on durable, tightly woven fabrics, but it may damage more delicate materials. When stain-removal directions call for tamping, the only tool you need is a small brush (a soft-bristled toothbrush is usually fine). Place the stained article on the work surface—no need for an absorbent pad. Hold the brush 2 or 3 inches above the stain and bring it down directly on the stain repeatedly in light strokes. You are using too much pressure if the bristles bend. Try to hit the stained area squarely with the tips of the bristles. You are more likely to damage the fabric if you hit it with the side of the brush. To avoid harming the fabric, stop tamping as soon as the spot is removed. Tightly woven fabrics of high-twist yarn are able to withstand more tamping than loosely woven fabrics of slight- or moderate-twist yarn.

CHAPTER 5
REMOVING SPOTS & STAINS

Procedures and products listed in this book have been carefully tested. To use the chart, first locate the "staining agent," or the substance that created the stain; these staining substances are listed in alphabetical order. Next, find the type of surface that the stain is on in the listing (also alphabetized at the top of each section). Then read the procedure listed.

Specific stain-removal techniques, including brushing, flushing, freezing, presoaking, pretreating, scraping, sponging, and tamping, are not described in detail each time they are listed on the chart. Refer to Chapter 4 for explanations of how to use these techniques properly.

Unless you know a surface is colorfast, can accurately identify the stain, and know which products are safe to use on the stain target, *always* pretest cleaning products on a hidden portion of the stained item. Even a common agent like water can leave marks that are impossible to remove. When using any stain-removing product, it is better to read the manufacturer's cautions and test the product's action on an inconspicuous spot (a hem, a hidden portion of carpet, etc.) than to ruin the stained surface.

Note: In most instances, the first few steps listed on the chart should completely remove a

fresh stain, making the remaining steps
unnecessary. However, be sure to follow the procedures in sequence until the stain is removed.

Alcoholic Beverages

**●Acetate ●Burlap ●Felt ●Fiberglass ●Rayon
●Rope ●Silk ●Triacetate ●Wool**
Blot up any excess liquid. Spray on a spot remover. Or, flush area with cool water. Apply a
Wet Spotter and a few drops of white vinegar.
Cover with an absorbent pad dampened with
the Wet Spotter and let stand as long as any
stain is being removed. Keep the stain and pad
moist, changing the pad as it picks up the stain.
Flush with cool water, blotting excess liquid
with a clean absorbent pad. Dry thoroughly.

**●Acrylic Fabric ●Cotton ●Linen ●Nylon ●Olefin
●Polyester ●Spandex**
Apply a spot remover. Or, sponge stain promptly
with cool water. If possible, presoak the stain
in cool water for at least 30 minutes or overnight. Work undiluted dishwashing or liquid
laundry detergent into stain. Rinse well. Launder as soon as possible. Old or ironed-in stains
may be impossible to remove.

**●Acrylic Plastic ●Aluminum ●Asphalt
●Chromium ●Copper ●Cork ●Enamel ●Glass
●Iron ●Ivory ●Jade ●Linoleum ●Paint/Flat
●Paint/Gloss ●Pearls ●Platinum ●Plexiglas
●Polyurethane ●Stainless Steel ●Tin ●Vinyl
Clothing ●Vinyl Tile ●Vinyl Wallcovering ●Zinc**

Wipe spill immediately with a cloth or sponge moistened with warm sudsy water. Rinse well and wipe dry.

●*Alabaster* ●*Marble*
Wipe immediately and thoroughly with a damp cloth. If a stain remains, make a poultice of water, chlorine bleach, and a mild powder laundry detergent and put it on the stain. Cover with a damp cloth. Let it stand until the stain is bleached out. Rinse thoroughly and dry.

●*Bamboo* ●*Cane* ●*Ceramic Glass/Tile* ●*Gold*
Wipe up spill immediately. Wash with a cloth dipped in a solution of warm water and mild pure soap with a few drops of ammonia added. Rinse with clear water and dry thoroughly.

●*Bluestone* ●*Brick* ●*Concrete* ●*Flagstone* ●*Granite* ●*Limestone* ●*Masonry Tile* ●*Sandstone* ●*Slate* ●*Terrazzo*
Wipe up spill immediately. Clean any residue with a solution of washing soda or all-purpose laundry detergent (do not use soap) and water. Rinse well. Allow to dry thoroughly.

●*Brass* ●*Bronze*
Wipe up spill immediately. Wash with a cloth dipped in a solution of hot water and a mild soap. Rinse with clear water and wipe thoroughly dry.

●*Carpet/Synthetic* ●*Carpet/Wool* ●*Foam Rubber*
After blotting up excess, apply a carpet stain remover. An alternative technique is to blot up excess moisture, working from the outside of the spill inward. Spray with a rug shampoo or

mix 1 teaspoon of a mild, non-alkali detergent in ½ pint lukewarm water. Add a small amount to the stain and blot until no more is removed. Mix 1 part white vinegar to 2 parts lukewarm water. Apply a small amount of the mixture and blot to neutralize any of the remaining stain. Place an absorbent pad over the stained area and weight it down for several hours. Allow to dry thoroughly.

●Fur/Natural ●Fur/Synthetic

For quick spot removal, use disposable cleaning cloths. Or, blot up spill immediately with a clean dry cloth. Try to prevent the hide or backing from getting wet. Mix dishwashing detergent in hot water and swish to make a great volume of suds. Dip a cloth in only the foam and gently rub with the nap. Rinse with another cloth dipped in clear water and wrung nearly dry. Allow to air dry away from heat.

●Grout

Wipe spill immediately. This should be all that is needed, but if the sealer on the grout is gone or old, try dipping a wet toothbrush into a little powdered cleaner, or apply a tile and grout cleaner. Gently scrub. Rinse thoroughly and allow to dry.

●Leather ●Suede

Blot up spill immediately. On leather, mix a solution of mild soap in lukewarm water. Swish to make a great volume of suds. Apply only the suds to suede or leather with a slightly damp cloth. Rub gently, but with vigor. Rub dry with a clean cloth. On leather only, condition with saddle soap.

●*Silver*
Wipe up excess immediately. Wash silver in hot sudsy water with a soft cloth. Rinse well in clear hot water. Wipe dry immediately to prevent tarnish.

●*Wallpaper*
Blot up excess immediately. Wipe stained area very gently with clear warm water—do not use detergent or soap—without over-wetting the paper. Strokes should overlap or wall may become streaked. Carefully pat dry.

●*Wood*
Wipe spill immediately. Rub stained area with a liquid or paste wax, boiled linseed oil, or a cloth dampened in water and a few drops of ammonia. Rewax the stained area.

Baby Food/Formula

●*Acetate* ●*Burlap* ●*Carpet/Synthetic* ●*Carpet/ Wool* ●*Fiberglass* ●*Rayon* ●*Rope* ●*Silk* ●*Triacetate* ●*Wool*
Blot up excess liquid or scrape excess solids from fabric. Sponge with a dry-cleaning solvent,

or apply a Dry Spotter to the stain and cover with an absorbent pad dampened with the Dry Spotter. Let it stand as long as any stain is being removed. Keep pad and stain moist, changing the pad as it picks up the stain. Flush with one of the recommended liquid solvents. Allow to dry completely.

●Acrylic Fabric ●Cotton ●Linen ●Nylon ●Olefin ●Polyester ●Spandex

Blot up or scrape excess material and rinse stain in cool water. Presoak for 30 minutes in an enzyme presoak. Launder immediately if possible. If not, flush with cool water and allow to dry thoroughly. If stain has dried, repeated laundering may be necessary.

●Acrylic Plastic ●Aluminum ●Asphalt ●Bamboo ●Cane ●Ceramic Glass/Tile ●Chromium ●Cork ●Enamel ●Glass ●Iron ●Linoleum ●Marble ●Paint/Flat ●Paint/Gloss ●Plexiglas ●Polyurethane ●Porcelain ●Stainless Steel ●Tin ●Vinyl Clothing ●Vinyl Tile ●Vinyl Wallcovering

Wipe up spills or excess matter immediately with a sponge dipped in warm sudsy water. Rinse with clear water. Some baby foods contain dyes that will stain if allowed to remain on these surfaces.

●Grout

Wipe up excess liquid or solids from grouting. If any stain remains, dip a wet toothbrush into a little powdered cleanser or apply a grout cleaner. Gently scrub the grout. Rinse with clear water.

●*Leather* ●*Suede*
Carefully blot up liquid or scrape excess matter from surface immediately. Mix a solution of mild soap in lukewarm water. Swish to create a great volume of suds. Apply only the foam with a sponge. Blot dry with a clean cloth. If stain persists, file gently with an emery board or very fine (grade 6/0-8/0) sandpaper. Work slowly and carefully, because the procedure removes a fine layer of the hide. To leather only, apply saddle soap to condition the leather.

●*Silver*
Wash silver immediately in hot sudsy water. Rinse in hot water and dry immediately with a soft cloth or silver polishing cloth to prevent tarnish.

●*Wallpaper*
Carefully blot up excess liquid or scrape excess solids. Try wiping with a cool damp cloth in even, overlapping strokes. Pat dry. If stain persists, try rubbing very gently with an artgum eraser or a stale piece of rye bread to soak up the oily residue.

●*Wood*
Immediately wipe excess liquid or matter with a damp sponge. Follow with a coat of wood cleaner, then apply a polish or wax.

Beer

(Follow procedures for Alcoholic Beverages.*)*

Beets

(Follow procedures for Berries.*)*

Berries (Blueberry, Cranberry, Raspberry, Strawberry)

●*Acetate* ●*Carpet/Synthetic* ●*Carpet/Wool* ●*Fiberglass* ●*Rayon* ●*Rope* ●*Silk* ●*Triacetate* ●*Wool*

Spray on fabric spot cleaner. If stain remains, sponge with cool water. Then sponge the area with lemon juice (or rub the cut sides of a slice of lemon over the stain). Flush with water. Blot as much excess liquid as possible and allow to dry. If stain still persists, apply a Wet Spotter. Cover with an absorbent pad moistened with Wet Spotter. Let stand as long as any stain is being removed. Change the pad as it picks up the stain. Keep the pad and stained area moist with Wet Spotter. Flush with water. If any trace of stain still appears, moisten the area with a solution of 1 cup warm water and 1 teaspoon of an enzyme presoak product—do not use on silk or wool. Cover with a clean absorbent pad that has been dipped in the solution and wrung almost dry. Let it stand for 30 minutes. Add enough solution to keep the stain and pad moist, but do not allow the wet area to spread.

When no more stain is visible, flush thoroughly with water and allow to air dry.

●Acrylic Fabric ●Modacrylic ●Nylon ●Olefin ●Polyester ●Spandex
Spray on a fabric spot cleaner. If stain remains, sponge with cool water immediately. Then sponge with lemon juice or rub a lemon slice over the stain. Flush with water. Blot as much excess liquid as possible and allow to dry. If any trace of stain still exists, presoak in a solution of 1 quart warm water, ½ teaspoon liquid dishwashing or laundry detergent, and 1 tablespoon white vinegar for 15 minutes. Rinse with water and launder if possible. If not, presoak in a solution of 1 quart warm water and 1 tablespoon of an enzyme presoak product, for 30 minutes. Rinse well with water and launder as soon as possible.

●Acrylic Plastic ●Aluminum ●Asphalt ●Bamboo ●Brass ●Bronze ●Cane ●Ceramic Glass/Tile ●Copper ●Enamel ●Glass ●Grout ●Iron ●Paint/Flat ● Paint/Gloss ●Plexiglas ●Polyurethane ●Porcelain Dishes ●Porcelain Fixtures ●Stainless Steel ●Vinyl Clothing ●Vinyl Wallcovering
Wipe up any excess spill with a cloth or sponge dipped in warm sudsy water. Rinse well and wipe dry.

●Bluestone ●Brick ●Concrete ●Flagstone ●Granite ●Masonry Tile ●Slate ●Terrazzo
Wipe up excess spill. Wash area with a solution of washing soda or detergent (not soap) and water. Use a soft cloth or soft-bristled brush. Rinse thoroughly with clear water and allow to dry.

●Cork ●Linoleum ●Vinyl Tile
Wipe up excess spill and wash the area with a solution of washing soda or detergent and water. Use a soft-bristled brush or cloth to scrub gently. Rinse thoroughly with clear water and allow to dry. If stain persists, wipe area with a cloth dampened in a solution of 1 tablespoon oxalic acid and 1 pint water. Rinse well and wipe dry. Repolish the surface if necessary.

●Cotton ●Linen
Test fabric for colorfastness. If color doesn't change, stretch the stain over a bowl; fasten in place with a rubber band. Pour boiling water through the fabric from the height of 2 or 3 feet. Avoid splatters. This procedure must be done immediately. If stain persists, soak in a solution of 1 quart warm water and ½ teaspoon detergent for 15 minutes. Rinse with water. Sponge the area with rubbing alcohol and launder if possible. If not, presoak in a solution of 1 quart warm water and 1 tablespoon of an enzyme presoak product for 30 minutes. Rinse well and launder.

●Leather ●Suede
Blot up any excess liquid. Mix a solution of mild soap in lukewarm water. Swish to create a great volume of suds. Apply only the foam with a sponge. Wipe with a clean dry cloth. On leather only, follow with saddle soap to condition the leather.

●Marble
After wiping up any excess liquid, wipe surface with a cloth or sponge dipped in warm sudsy water. Rinse well and wipe dry. If any stain or

discoloration remains, mix a poultice of water, powdered detergent, and chlorine bleach. Apply a thick paste to the stain and cover with a damp cloth to retard evaporation. When the stain has been bleached out, rinse thoroughly and dry.

●Silver
Wash silver as soon as possible in hot sudsy water. Rinse in hot water and dry immediately with a soft cloth to prevent tarnish.

●Wood
Mix dishwashing detergent in hot water and swish to make a great volume of suds. Dip a cloth in only the foam and apply to berry stain. Rinse with a clean cloth dampened with clear water. If any stain remains, rub the area with a cloth dampened in a solution of 1 tablespoon oxalic acid to 1 pint water. Rinse well and wipe dry. Wax or polish as soon as possible.

Blood

●Acetate ●Burlap ●Fiberglass ●Rayon ●Rope ●Silk ●Triacetate ●Wool
Treat the stain as soon as possible, as set blood stains can be extremely difficult to remove. Sponge the stain with cold water. If the blood is still wet, this step should remove it. If any stain remains, apply a Wet Spotter and a few drops of ammonia (but do not use ammonia on silk and wool). Cover with an absorbent pad dampened with the Wet Spotter and ammonia. Let it stand as long as any stain is being re-

moved, changing the pad as it picks up the stain. Keep the stain and pad moist with the Wet Spotter and ammonia. Flush thoroughly with cool water, making sure to remove all traces of ammonia. If stain persists, moisten it with a solution of ½ teaspoon of an enzyme presoak product—except on silk or wool—and ½ cup warm water. Cover the stain with an absorbent pad dampened slightly with the enzyme solution. Let it stand for 30 minutes. Add more solution to keep the stain moist and warm, but do not let the wet area spread. Flush with water and dry thoroughly.

●Acrylic Fabric ●Cotton ●Linen ●Nylon ●Olefin ●Polyester ●Spandex
Fresh blood stains can usually be removed by a thorough laundering in cold water. If any stain remains, soak it in a solution of 1 quart warm water, ½ teaspoon dishwashing or liquid laundry detergent, and 1 tablespoon ammonia for 15 minutes. Tamp or scrape, blotting occasionally with an absorbent pad. Continue as long as any stain is being removed. Rinse well with water, making sure to remove all traces of the ammonia. If stain persists, presoak in a solution of 1 quart warm water and 1 tablespoon of an enzyme presoak. After 30 minutes, rinse well, then dry or launder.

●Acrylic Plastic ●Aluminum ●Asphalt ●Brass ●Bronze ●Ceramic Glass/Tile ●Chrominum ●Copper ●Coral ●Cork ●Enamel ●Glass ●Gold ●Iron ●Ivory ●Jade ●Linoleum ●Opal ●Paint/ Flat ●Paint/Gloss ●Pearls ●Pewter ●Platinum ●Plexiglas ●Polyurethane ●Porcelain ●Stain-

less Steel •*Tin* •*Vinyl Clothing* •*Vinyl Tile*
•*Vinyl Wallcovering* •*Zinc*
Wipe up stain with a sponge or cloth dipped in cool water or warm sudsy water. Dry with a clean cloth.

•*Alabaster* •*Marble*
Wipe stain with a sponge dipped in cold water. If stain remains, mix a poultice of water, powdered detergent, and chlorine bleach. Apply it thickly to the stain and cover with a damp cloth to retard drying. When the stain has been bleached out, rinse thoroughly and dry.

•*Bamboo* •*Cane*
Wash with a cloth or brush dipped in warm soapy water to which a few drops of ammonia have been added. Rinse with clear water and dry.

•*Bluestone* •*Brick* •*Concrete* •*Flagstone* •*Granite* •*Limestone* •*Masonry Tile* •*Sandstone* •*Slate* •*Terrazzo*
Try wiping up the stain with a sponge dipped in cool water. If any stain remains, wash or brush stain with a solution of washing soda or detergent in warm water. Rinse well and allow to dry.

•*Carpet/Synthetic* •*Carpet/Wool* •*Foam Rubber*
Apply a carpet stain remover to the stained area. Another way to remove blood is to mix 1 teaspoon of mild, non-alkali detergent with ½ pint lukewarm water. Add a small amount to the stain and blot the liquid. Do not force the stain further into the fibers. Continue blotting until no more stain is removed. If stain remains, add

1 tablespoon ammonia to 1 cup water (do not use on wool), sponge stain, and blot liquid. Continue until no more stain is removed. Place an absorbent pad over the damp area and weight it down. When no more liquid is drawn out, remove the pad and allow it to air dry thoroughly.

●*Fur/Natural* ●*Fur/Synthetic*
Blot up excess. Wring a cloth in the suds of a mild detergent to which a few drops of ammonia have been added. Rub with the nap, taking care not to over-wet the pelt or backing. To rinse, dip a cloth in cool water, wring almost dry, and stroke with the nap. Air dry away from heat.

●*Grout*
Wipe the stain with a sponge dipped in cool water. If any remains, dip a wet toothbrush into a little baking soda or powdered cleanser, or apply a tile and grout cleaner and gently scrub the grout. Rinse thoroughly and dry.

●*Leather* ●*Suede*
Mix a solution of mild soap in lukewarm water. Swish to create a great volume of suds. Apply only the foam with a sponge and gently rub the stained area, taking care not to spread the stain. Wipe dry with a clean soft cloth. On leather only, follow with saddle soap to condition the leather.

●*Silver*
Wash silver in hot sudsy water. Rinse in hot water and wipe dry immediately with a soft cloth to prevent tarnish.

●Wallpaper

Blood can permanently stain wallpaper. Try dipping a cloth in cool water, wringing until damp, and gently sponging the area, taking care not to spread the stain. Overlap the strokes slightly to prevent streaking. Gently pat dry.

●Wood

Wipe the stain with a cloth dipped in cool water. Wipe dry immediately and polish or wax as usual.

Catsup

●Acetate ●Burlap ●Carpet/Synthetic ●Carpet/Wool ●Fiberglass ●Rayon ●Rope ●Silk ●Triacetate ●Wool

Gently scrape any excess from fabric. Sponge with cleaning fluid or treat silk by applying a spot remover. Apply a Dry Spotter to the stain and cover with an absorbent pad dampened with the Dry Spotter. Keep the stain and pad moist. Let it stand as long as any stain is being removed. Change the pad as it picks up the stain. When no more stain is being removed, flush with cleaning fluid or reapply a spot lifter on silk. Allow to dry. If any stain remains, moisten it with a solution of ½ teaspoon of an enzyme presoak product (do not use on silk and wool) and ½ cup warm water. Cover with a clean pad that has been dipped in the enzyme presoak solution and squeezed nearly dry. Let it stand for 30 minutes, adding more solution as needed to keep the area warm and moist, but do not let the wet area spread. Flush with water and allow to dry. On carpets, place a clean dry pad over the area and weight it down. When no more liquid is being absorbed, allow to air dry thoroughly.

●Acrylic Fabric ●Cotton ●Linen ●Modacrylic ●Nylon ●Olefin ●Polyester ●Spandex
Scrape as much of the excess as possible with a spatula. Apply a Wet Spotter and work into the fabric. Rinse thoroughly with water and launder. If laundering must wait, and there is any stain remaining, apply an enzyme presoak paste made from an enzyme presoak product and let it work awhile, keeping the paste moist. Thoroughly rinse area to remove all traces of enzyme presoak paste. Allow to dry and launder as soon as possible.

●Acrylic Plastic ●Aluminum ●Asphalt ●Bamboo ●Bronze ●Cane ●Ceramic Glass/Tile ●Chromium ●Copper ●Cork ●Enamel ●Glass ●Gold ●Iron ●Ivory ●Linoleum ●Paint/Flat ●Paint/Gloss ●Pewter ●Plexiglas ●Polyurethane ●Porcelain Dishes ●Stainless Steel ●Tin ●Vinyl Clothing ●Vinyl Tile ●Vinyl Wallcovering ●Zinc
Wipe up spills as soon as possible—the tomato in catsup can permanently stain many of these surfaces—with a cloth or sponge dipped in warm sudsy water. Rinse with clean water and wipe dry.

●Alabaster ●Bluestone ●Concrete ●Flagstone ●Granite ●Limestone ●Marble ●Masonry Tile

•Sandstone •Slate •Terrazzo
Remove excess. Wipe with a cloth dipped in a solution of washing soda or detergent in warm water. If any stain remains, mix a poultice of water, mild bleach, and a powdered detergent and apply to the stained area. Cover with a damp cloth to retard evaporation. When stain is gone, rinse well and wipe dry.

•Leather •Suede
Mix a solution of mild soap in lukewarm water. Swish to create a great volume of suds. Apply only the foam with a sponge. Wipe dry with a clean cloth. On leather only, follow with saddle soap to condition the leather.

•Silver
Take care of silver as soon as possible, as tomato can pit the metal. Wash silver in hot soapy water. Rinse in hot water and wipe dry with a clean soft cloth.

•Wallpaper
Wipe immediately, as catsup often permanently stains wallpaper. Use a damp cloth or sponge, overlapping strokes to prevent streaks. Gently pat dry.

•Wood
Catsup spills usually occur on wood (tabletops, etc.) that has a treated surface, such as polyurethane sealer. Wiping these surfaces with a damp cloth is sufficient to remove the spill. Nontreated surfaces should be wiped immediately with a cloth dipped in warm sudsy water, rinsed with a clean damp cloth, wiped dry, and polished or waxed as usual.

Cherry

●*Acetate* ●*Carpet/Synthetic* ●*Carpet/Wool*
●*Fiberglass* ●*Rayon* ●*Rope* ●*Silk* ●*Triacetate*
●*Wool*

Spray on a fabric spot cleaner. If stain remains,
sponge with cool water. Then sponge the area
with lemon juice (or rub the cut sides of a slice
of lemon over the stain). Flush with water. Blot
as much excess liquid as possible and allow to
dry. If stain still persists, apply a Wet Spotter.
Cover with an absorbent pad moistened with
Wet Spotter. Let stand as long as any stain is
being removed. Change the pad as it picks up
the stain. Keep the pad and stained area moist
with Wet Spotter. Flush with water. If any trace
of stain still appears, moisten the area with a
solution of 1 cup warm water and 1 teaspoon
of an enzyme presoak product—do not use on
silk or wool. Cover with a clean absorbent pad
that has been dipped in the solution and wrung
almost dry. Let it stand for 30 minutes. Add
enough solution to keep the stain and pad
moist, but do not allow the wet area to spread.
When no more stain is visible, flush thoroughly
with water and allow to air dry.

●*Acrylic Fabric* ●*Modacrylic* ●*Nylon* ●*Olefin*
●*Polyester* ●*Spandex*

Spray on a fabric spot cleaner. If stain remains,
sponge with cool water immediately. Then
sponge with lemon juice or rub a lemon slice
over the stain. Flush with water. Blot as much
excess liquid as is possible and allow to dry. If
any trace of stain still exists, presoak in a sol-

ution of 1 quart warm water, ½ teaspoon liquid dishwashing or laundry detergent, and 1 table-spoon white vinegar for 15 minutes. Rinse with water and launder if possible. If not, soak in a solution of 1 quart water and 1 tablespoon of an enzyme presoak product for 30 minutes. Rinse well with water and launder as soon as possible.

•*Acrylic Plastic* •*Aluminum* •*Asphalt* •*Bamboo*
•*Brass* •*Bronze* •*Cane* •*Ceramic Glass/Tile*
•*Copper* •*Enamel* •*Glass* •*Grout* •*Iron*
•*Paint/Flat* •*Paint/Gloss* •*Plexiglas*
•*Polyurethane* •*Porcelain Fixtures*
•*Stainless Steel* •*Vinyl Clothing*
•*Vinyl Wallcovering*
Wipe up any excess spill with a cloth or sponge dipped in warm sudsy water. Rinse well and wipe dry.

•*Bluestone* •*Brick* •*Concrete* •*Flagstone*
•*Granite* •*Masonry Tile* •*Slate* •*Terrazzo*
Wipe up excess spill. Wash area with a solution of washing soda or detergent (not soap) and water. Use a soft cloth or soft-bristled brush. Rinse thoroughly with clear water and allow to dry.

•*Cork* •*Linoleum* •*Vinyl Tile*
Wipe up excess spill and wash the area with a solution of washing soda or detergent and water. Use a soft-bristled brush or cloth to scrub gently. Rinse thoroughly with clear water and allow to dry. If stain persists, wipe area with a cloth dampened in a solution of 1 tablespoon oxalic acid and 1 pint water. Rinse well and wipe dry. Repolish the surface if necessary.

●Cotton ●Linen

Test fabric for colorfastness. If color doesn't change, stretch the stain over a bowl; fasten in place with a rubber band. Pour boiling water through the fabric from the height of 2 or 3 feet. Avoid splatters. This procedure must be done immediately. If stain persists, soak in a solution of 1 quart warm water and ½ teaspoon detergent for 15 minutes. Rinse with water. Sponge area with rubbing alcohol and launder if possible. If not, presoak in a solution of 1 quart warm water and 1 tablespoon of an enzyme presoak product for 30 minutes. Rinse well and launder.

●Leather ●Suede

Blot up any excess liquid. Mix solution of mild soap in lukewarm water. Swish to create a great volume of suds. Apply only the foam with a sponge. Wipe with a clean dry cloth. On leather only, follow with saddle soap to condition the leather.

●Marble

After wiping up any excess liquid, wipe surface with a cloth or sponge dipped in warm sudsy water. Rinse well and wipe dry. If any stain or discoloration remains, mix a poultice of water, powdered detergent, and chlorine bleach. Apply a thick paste to the stain and cover with a damp cloth to retard evaporation. When the stain has been bleached out, rinse thoroughly and dry.

●Silver

Wash silver as soon as possible in hot sudsy water. Rinse in hot water and dry immediately with a soft cloth to prevent tarnish.

●Wood

Mix dishwashing detergent in hot water and swish to make a great volume of suds. Dip a cloth in only the foam and apply to the stain. Rinse with a clean cloth dampened with clear water. If any stain remains, rub the area with a cloth dampened in a solution of 1 tablespoon oxalic acid to 1 pint water. Rinse well and wipe dry. Wax or polish as soon as possible.

Chewing Gum

●Acetate ●Acrylic Fabric ●Burlap ●Carpet/Synthetic ●Carpet/Wool ●Cotton ●Fiberglass ●Linen ●Modacrylic ●Nylon ●Olefin ●Polyester ●Rayon ●Silk ●Spandex ●Triacetate ●Wool

Freeze until gum gets hard. Carefully scrape or rub the matter from the fabric. Sponge with a dry-cleaning solvent. Apply a Dry Spotter to the stain and cover with an absorbent pad dampened with the Dry Spotter. Let it stand as long as any stain is being removed. Change the pad as it picks up the stain. Keep the stain and pad moist with the Dry Spotter. Flush with one of the dry-cleaning solvents. If stain remains, reapply the Dry Spotter and cover. Check the stain every 5 minutes and press hard against the stain when you are checking. Continue the alternate soaking and pressing until all the stain has been removed. Flush with the dry-cleaning solvent. Dry.

●Acrylic Plastic ●Aluminum Asphalt ●Paint/ Flat ●Paint/Gloss ●Plexiglas ●Polyurethane ●Vinyl Clothing

Freeze until gum gets hard. Carefully scrape or rub the substance from the surface. With a clean cloth dipped in warm sudsy water, wipe the surface until all traces of the gum have been removed. Rinse well and wipe dry.

●Bamboo ●Cane

Freeze until gum gets hard. Carefully scrape any excess. Wipe with a cloth dipped in a solution of warm sudsy water to which a few drops of ammonia have been added. Rinse well and allow to dry.

●Felt

Since felt is not woven, but rather fused together, take every precaution in removing any excess gum as chunks of the felt may come with it. Freeze to harden the remainder and gently brush with a sponge or fine-bristled brush (such as a toothbrush). This should remove any excess that remains on the surface. In extreme cases, very carefully rub a razor blade with the nap. This will also remove some of the felt fibers. If stain persists, make a paste of cornmeal and a small amount of water and apply it to the stain. Give it plenty of time to work. When it is dry, carefully brush it off with the nap.

●Fur/Natural ●Fur/Synthetic

Take care not to remove the fur when removing the gum. Freeze to harden the remainder and gently rub it with a dry sponge or brush to remove the remaining gum. Another effective treatment is to dampen a sponge or cloth in the suds of a mild detergent and wipe in the direction of the nap to remove any sugary residue. Take care not to over-wet the pelt or backing. Allow to air dry.

●Leather

Carefully scrape excess gum. Mix a solution of mild soap in lukewarm water. Swish to create a great volume of suds. Apply only the foam with a sponge and scrub gently until matter is removed. Dry with a clean cloth. Follow with saddle soap to condition the leather.

●Linoleum ●Vinyl Tile ●Vinyl Wallcovering

Freeze the gum to harden it. Use a dull tool such as a metal spatula to scrape the brittle matter without gouging the surface. If there is any residue, try rubbing it with a cloth dipped in a cleaning fluid. Wipe gingerly, then rub with extra fine (number 000) steel wool. Wash the area and wax when dry.

●Suede

Very carefully scrape to remove excess. Gently rub an artgum eraser over the remaining substance. If any stain remains, apply a treatment of a suede cleaner. If there is still some remaining, cautiously rub the spot with an emery board or extra fine (number 000) sandpaper. In either case, you are removing a fine layer of the hide, so work slowly and carefully.

●Wood

Take special precautions in removing any excess so as not to remove any of the finish. Rub gently with a cloth dipped in the suds of hot soapy water. Wipe dry immediately and polish or wax as usual.

Chocolate/Cocoa

●*Acetate* ●*Burlap* ●*Fiberglass* ●*Rayon* ●*Rope* ●*Silk* ●*Triacetate* ●*Wool*

Blot up any excess, or scrape any matter from the surface. Flush the stain with club soda to prevent setting. Sponge the stain with a dry-cleaning solvent. Then apply a Dry Spotter to the stain and cover with an absorbent pad dampened with the Dry Spotter. Keep the stain and pad moist with the Dry Spotter. Let it stand as long as any any stain is being removed. Change the pad as it picks up the stain. Flush with one of the dry-cleaning solvents. If a stain remains, moisten it with a solution of 1 cup of warm water and 1 teaspoon of an enzyme presoak—but do not use on silk or wool. Cover with a clean pad that has been dipped in the solution and wrung almost dry. Let it stand at least 30 minutes. Add more solution if needed to keep the stain warm and moist, but do not allow the wet area to spread. When the stain is lifted, flush thoroughly with water and allow to dry.

●*Acrylic Fabric* ●*Cotton* ●*Linen* ●*Nylon* ●*Modacrylic* ●*Olefin* ●*Polyester* ●*Spandex*

Wipe up as much excess as possible without driving the stain further into the fibers. Flush the stain with club soda. Sponge the area with a dry-cleaning solvent. Apply a Dry Spotter to the stain and cover with an absorbent pad dampened with the Dry Spotter. Keep the stain moist with Dry Spotter. Let it stand as long as any stain is being lifted. Change the pad as it picks up the stain. Flush with one of the liquid dry-

cleaning solvents. If any stain remains, apply a
few drops of ammonia to the stain, then tamp
or scrape. Keep the stain moist with the detergent and ammonia and blot occasionally with
an absorbent pad. Flush well with water to remove all traces of ammonia. Allow to dry or
launder as usual.

●*Acrylic Plastic* ●*Aluminum* ●*Asphalt* ●*Bamboo*
●*Brass* ●*Bronze* ●*Cane* ●*Ceramic Glass/Tile*
●*Copper* ●*Cork* ●*Enamel* ●*Glass* ●*Gold* ●*Iron*
●*Ivory* ●*Jade* ●*Paint/Flat* ●*Paint/Gloss* ●*Pewter*
●*Plexiglas* ●*Polyurethane* ●*Porcelain* ●*Stain-
less Steel* ●*Tin* ●*Vinyl Clothing* ●*Vinyl Tile*
●*Vinyl Wallcovering* ●*Zinc*
Scrape to remove excess. Wipe the surface with
a cloth dipped in warm sudsy water. Rinse well
and wipe dry.

●*Alabaster* ●*Marble*
Carefully scrape excess. Wipe with a clean cloth
dipped in a solution of washing soda or detergent and water. Rinse well and wipe dry. If any
stain remains, mix a few drops of ammonia with
1 cup 3% hydrogen peroxide. Soak a white blotter with the solution and place it over the stain.
Weight it down with a heavy object. Continue
applying the solution until the oil has been
drawn out and any stain bleached.

●*Bluestone* ●*Brick* ●*Concrete* ●*Flagstone*
●*Granite* ●*Limestone* ●*Masonry Tile*
●*Sandstone* ●*Slate* ●*Terrazzo*
Scrape to remove excess, taking care not to
gouge the surface. Wash with a solution of washing soda or detergent (never use soap) and
water. Use a cloth or gentle brush. Rinse
thoroughly with clear water and allow to dry.

●Carpet/Synthetic ●Carpet/Wool

Blot up or scrape as much of the excess as possible. To prevent setting stain, flush with club soda. Try an application of carpet stain remover or a concentrated solution of a non-alkali carpet shampoo. After drying and vacuuming, if stain remains, mix 1 tablespoon ammonia to 1 cup water and carefully drop small amounts onto the stain. (On wool carpets, test in an inconspicuous corner first, as ammonia can harm wool.) Blot with an absorbent pad. Flush area rugs or sponge carpeting with clear water. It is important to remove all traces of ammonia. Place a clean absorbent pad over the area and weight it down. When no more liquid is being absorbed, allow it to thoroughly air dry.

●Felt ●Fur/Natural ●Fur/Synthetic

Gently scrape to remove excess. Mix a mild soap in hot water and swish to make a great volume of suds. Dip a cloth in only the foam and apply. Rinse by wiping with a clean cloth dampened with clear water. If a grease stain remains, powder the stain with an absorbent such as cornmeal. Give it plenty of time to work. Gently brush it out. Take care not to force the absorbent further into the hairs. Repeat if necessary.

●Grout

Wipe excess with a cloth dipped in warm sudsy water. If any stain remains, dip a wet toothbrush into baking soda or powdered cleanser, or apply a tile and grout cleaner and gently scrub the spot. Rinse well and wipe dry.

●Leather ●Suede

Gently scrape excess from the surface. Mix solution of mild soap in lukewarm water. Swish to create a great volume of suds. Apply only the foam with a sponge. Wipe dry with a clean cloth. If a stain remains, powder it with an absorbent such as cornmeal. Give it plenty of time to work. Gently brush it off. Repeat if necessary; on leather only, follow with saddle soap to condition the leather.

●Silver
Wash silver in hot sudsy water. Rinse thoroughly in hot water. Wipe dry immediately with a clean soft cloth to prevent tarnish.

●Wood
Mix dishwashing detergent in hot water and swish to make a great volume of suds. Dip a cloth in only the foam and apply. Rinse with a clean cloth dampened with clear water. Polish or wax as usual.

Coffee

●Acetate ●Fiberglass ●Rayon ●Triacetate
Blot up with a clean cloth. Sponge the stain with water. Apply a fabric spot cleaner or a Wet Spotter and a few drops of white vinegar. Cover with an absorbent pad dampened with the Wet Spotter. Keep the stain and pad moist with the Wet Spotter and vinegar. Let it stand as long as any stain is being removed. Change the pad as it picks up the stain. Flush with water. Repeat until no more stain is removed. If a stain remains, moisten it with a solution of 1 teaspoon of an enzyme presoak and 1 cup warm water. Cover with a clean pad that has been dipped in

the solution and wrung almost dry. Let it stand for at least 30 minutes. Add more solution if needed to keep the area warm and moist, but do not allow the wet area to spread. When the stain is removed, or no more is being lifted, flush thoroughly with water and allow to dry.

●*Acrylic Fabric* ●*Modacrylic* ●*Nylon* ●*Olefin* ●*Polyester* ●*Spandex*

Blot up any excess with a clean cloth. Presoak the stain in a solution of 1 quart warm water, ½ teaspoon dishwashing detergent, and 1 tablespoon white vinegar for 15 minutes. Rinse with water. Sponge the remaining stain with rubbing alcohol and launder if possible. If not, presoak it in a solution of 1 quart warm water and 1 tablespoon of an enzyme presoak for 30 minutes. Rinse well with water. Allow to dry, but launder as soon as possible.

●*Acrylic Plastic* ●*Aluminum* ●*Asphalt* ●*Bamboo* ●*Brass* ●*Bronze* ●*Cane* ●*Ceramic Glass/Tile* ●*Copper* ●*Cork* ●*Enamel* ●*Glass* ●*Gold* ●*Grout* ●*Iron* ●*Ivory* ●*Jade* ●*Linoleum* ●*Paint/Flat* ●*Paint/Gloss* ●*Pewter* ●*Plexiglas* ●*Polyurethane* ●*Stainless Steel* ●*Tin* ●*Vinyl Clothing* ●*Vinyl Tile* ●*Vinyl Wallcovering* ●*Zinc*

Blot up any excess. Wipe the surface with a cloth or sponge dipped in warm sudsy water. Rinse well and wipe dry.

●*Alabaster* ●*Marble*

Blot up any excess. Wipe the surface with a cloth dipped in a solution of washing soda or detergent and water. Rinse well and wipe dry. If a stain remains, mix a few drops of ammonia with 1 cup 3% hydrogen peroxide. Soak a white blotter with the solution and place it over the stain. Cover it with a piece of glass or other heavy object. Continue applying the solution until the oil has been drawn out and any remaining stain is bleached out.

●Bluestone ●Brick ●Concrete ●Flagstone ●Granite ●Limestone ●Masonry Tile ●Sandstone ●Slate ●Terrazzo
Mix a solution of washing soda or a detergent in water. Gently brush stain away. Wash with clear water and allow to dry.

●Burlap ●Silk ●Wool
Blot up excess. Sponge the stain with water. Apply a fabric spot cleaner or a Wet Spotter and a few drops of white vinegar. Cover with an absorbent pad dampened with the Wet Spotter. Let it stand as long as any stain is being lifted. Change the pad as it picks up the stain. Keep the stain and pad moist with the Wet Spotter and vinegar. Flush with water. Repeat until no more stain is being removed. If any stain remains, apply rubbing alcohol to the stain and cover with an absorbent pad dampened with alcohol. Let it stand as long as it is picking up stain, changing the pad as it does. Keep the stain and pad moist with alcohol. Flush with water. For stubborn or old stain, try moistening the stain with a solution of 1 tablespoon of an enzyme presoak product and 1 cup of warm water—use only on burlap. Cover with a clean pad dipped in the solution and squeezed almost dry. Let it stand for at least 30 minutes. Add more solution as needed to keep the area warm and moist, but do not allow the wet area to spread. When the stain is lifted, flush thoroughly with water.

•Carpet/Synthetic •Carpet/Wool •Foam Rubber
Blot up what you can. Apply a carpet stain remover. Flush the stain with a solution of 1 quart warm water, ½ teaspoon liquid laundry or dishwashing detergent, and 1 tablespoon white vinegar. Blot with a clean pad and rinse well with water. If the stain remains, try flushing it with a solution of 1 quart warm water and 1 tablespoon enzyme presoak (do not use on wool). Blot and flush alternately until no more stain is left. Sponge the area well with water. Blot all excess liquid and place a clean pad over the area and weight it down. When no more is being absorbed, allow the area to thoroughly air dry.

•Cotton •Linen
Blot up excess. Pretreat with laundry soil and stain remover, then launder immediately. If that is not possible, soak the stain in a solution of 1 quart warm water and ½ teaspoon dishwashing detergent for 15 minutes. Rinse well with water. Next, sponge the stain with rubbing alcohol. Rinse and allow to dry. If the stain remains, presoak it in a solution of warm water and an enzyme presoak product for 30 minutes. Rinse well with water and dry. Launder as soon as possible.

Another method that has worked is to stretch the stained area over a bowl and secure with a rubber band. Pour boiling water through the stain from a height of 2 to 3 feet. Stand back to avoid splatters. Although cotton and linen can stand boiling water, some of the finishes and colors used on the fabrics might be damaged by such harsh treatment. Be sure to test on a inconspicuous corner first.

•*Felt* •*Fur/Natural* •*Fur/Synthetic*

Blot up what you can without forcing the stain further into the fibers. Mix a mild soap in hot water and swish to make a great volume of suds. Dip a cloth in only the foam and apply. Rinse with a cloth dipped in clear water and wrung nearly dry. If an oily residue remains, powder the stain with an absorbent such as cornmeal. Don't push the powder into the fibers or pelt. Give it plenty of time to work. Gently brush or shake it out. Repeat if necessary. Make sure the material is dry before applying powder.

•*Leather* •*Suede*

Carefully blot up excess liquid. Mix a solution of mild soap in lukewarm water. Swish to create a great volume of suds. Apply only the foam with a sponge. Wipe dry with a clean dry cloth. If an oily stain remains, powder the stain with an absorbent such as cornmeal. Give it plenty of time to work. Gently brush it off. Repeat if necessary. On leather only, follow with saddle soap to condition the leather.

•*Porcelain Dishes* •*Porcelain Fixtures*

Clean the stain by washing it in warm sudsy water or wiping it with a cloth dipped in warm sudsy water. Rinse well and wipe it dry. To remove old stain from the bottom of cups, dip a soft, damp cloth into baking soda and wipe any remaining stain. Rinse well and dry.

•*Silver*

Wash silver in hot soapy water. Rinse in hot water and wipe dry immediately with a soft cloth.

•Wood
Gently wipe the surface with a cloth dipped in the suds of a mild detergent and water. Rinse well with a clean cloth dampened with clear water. Polish or wax the wood as soon as possible.

Cosmetics

(See Eyeliner/Eye Pencil/Eyeshadow, Lipstick.)

Crayon

•Acetate •Burlap •Fiberglass •Rayon •Rope •Silk •Triacetate •Wool/nonwashable
Gently scrape to remove excess matter. Place an absorbent pad under the stain and flush with a dry cleaning solvent. Allow to dry. Repeat if necessary.

•Acrylic Fabric •Cotton •Linen •Modacrylic •Nylon •Olefin Polyester •Spandex •Wool/washable
Scrape to remove the excess. Place the stain between two pieces of white blotting paper and press with a warm iron. Change the papers as the stain is absorbed. This stain can easily spread, so use care while pressing. On colorfast white cotton or linen, try pouring boiling water through the stain. After using either method, allow fabric to dry. If any trace remains, flush it with a dry-cleaning solvent. If any dye re-

mains, sponge it with 1 part rubbing alcohol (do not use on acrylic or modacrylic) in 2 parts water. Rinse well with clear water an allow to dry.

●*Acrylic Plastic* ●*Alabaster* ●*Aluminum* ●*Bamboo* ●*Bluestone* ●*Brass* ●*Brick* ●*Bronze* ●*Cane* ●*Ceramic Glass/Tile* ●*Concrete* ● *Copper* ●*Enamel* ●*Flagstone* ●*Glass* ●*Gold* ●*Granite* ●*Grout* ●*Iron* ●*Ivory* ●*Jade* ●*Limestone* ●*Marble* ●*Paint/Flat* ●*Paint/Gloss* ●*Pewter* ●*Plexiglas* ●*Polyurethane* ●*Porcelain* ●*Sandstone* ●*Slate* ●*Stainless Steel* ●*Terrazzo* ●*Tin* ●*Vinyl Clothing* ●*Vinyl Tile*

Gently scrape any excess crayon from the surface. Take care not to scratch the surface. This should be sufficient to remove the stain. Wipe with a sponge dipped in a solution of washing soda or detergent (not soap) and water. Rinse well and wipe dry.

●*Asphalt* ●*Cork* ●*Linoleum*

Treat these surfaces by using a metal spatula to gently scrape the surface; take care not to gouge it.

●*Carpet/Synthetic* ●*Carpet/Wool*

Gently scrape what you can from the surface. Add a small amount (to prevent damaging the carpet's backing) of dry-cleaning solvent and blot with an absorbent pad. Continue until no more stain is removed. If a dye remains, dilute 1 part rubbing alcohol with 2 parts water and test on an inconspicuous place. If the carpet is colorfast, apply the solution to the stain in small amounts, blotting well after each application. Allow to dry.

●*Felt*
Very carefully scrape the residue off, taking care not to pull out the fibers. If any residue remains, try brushing gently with a stiff-bristled brush. In extreme cases, use a razor blade to gently scrape the excess. Use this as a last resort as it will remove some of the fibers.

●*Leather* ●*Suede*
With a dull knife or your fingernail, gently scrape up the crayon. If any stain remains, mix a thick paste of fuller's earth and water and apply it to the stain. Carefully brush it off when dry. Repeat if necessary. When the stain has been removed, on leather only, follow with saddle soap to condition the leather.

●*Silver*
Scrape any excess material with your fingernail or nonmetal utensil until no more can be removed. Wash the silver in hot soapy water. Rinse in hot water and wipe dry.

●*Wallpaper*
Rub the crayon marks lightly with a mildly abrasive bar cleaner, rubbing in several directions if the wallpaper is textured. An alternate method is to spray spot lifter onto the stain. Or, lightly rub the stain with a dry soap-filled steel wool pad. If stain persists, rub very gently with baking soda sprinkled on a damp cloth. Wipe away any residue with a damp cloth and dry.

●*Wood*
Rub the crayon marks with a mildly abrasive bar cleaner, then polish or wax the wood. Or, gently remove any material by scraping with a

dull knife or your fingernail. Polish any remains with a chamois cloth.

Dye
(except red and yellow)

●Acetate ●Carpet/Synthetic ●Fiberglass ●Rayon ●Triacetate
Sponge with water. Spray on fabric spot cleaner. Then apply a Wet Spotter and a few drops of white vinegar. Use an absorbent pad dampened with Wet Spotter to blot occasionally. Keep the stain moist with Wet Spotter and vinegar. When no more stain can be blotted, flush with water. If stain persists, apply more Wet Spotter and a few drops of ammonia. Cover the stain this time with an absorbent pad and allow it to remain as long as any stain is being lifted. Keep stain and pad moist with Wet Spotter and ammonia. Flush with water and allow to dry.

●Acrylic Fabric ●Modacrylic ●Nylon ●Olefin ●Polyester ●Spandex
Presoak in a solution of 1 quart warm water, ½ teaspoon liquid dishwashing or laundry detergent, and 1 tablespoon white vinegar for 15 minutes. Rinse well and launder if possible. If not, presoak in solution of 1 quart warm water and 1 tablespoon of an enzyme presoak for 30 minutes. Rinse well and launder as soon as possible. If stain still remains, mix a solution of 1 tablespoon ammonia to 1 cup water. Be sure to test on a hidden seam first, then carefully, using

an eyedropper, drop solution onto stain. Blot with an absorbent pad. Flush with clear water. Place an absorbent pad over the stain and weight it down. When no more liquid is absorbed, allow it to thoroughly air dry.

•Acrylic Plastic •Aluminum •Bamboo •Cane •Ceramic Glass/Tile •Glass •Paint/Flat •Paint/Gloss •Plexiglas •Polyurethane •Vinyl Clothing •Vinyl Wallcovering
Immediately wipe up the spill with a cloth or sponge dipped in warm sudsy water. Rinse well and wipe dry.

•Alabaster •Marble
Immediately wipe up the spill with a cloth or sponge dipped in warm sudsy water. Rinse well and wipe dry. If stain persists, soak an absorbent pad in rubbing alcohol, wrung almost dry, and place over the stain. Wait 5 minutes and appply an absorbent pad soaked in ammonia and squeezed nearly dry. Alternate alcohol and ammonia pads until stain has been removed. Wipe surface with a cloth moistened with cool clear water and wipe dry with a clean cloth.

•Asphalt •Cork •Linoleum •Vinyl Tile
Wipe up any excess with a cloth or sponge dipped in warm sudsy water. Rinse well and wipe dry. If a stain persists, cover the stain with an absorbent pad soaked in rubbing alcohol. Let it remain in place for several minutes, then wipe the area with a cloth dampened with ammonia—do not use ammonia on linoleum or vinyl floor tile. Rinse well with a cloth dipped in warm sudsy water and rewipe with a cloth dampened with clear water. Allow to dry and polish or wax the surface.

- **Bluestone** • **Brick** • **Concrete** • **Flagstone**
- **Granite** • **Limestone** • **Masonry Tile**
- **Sandstone** • **Slate** • **Terrazzo**

Wipe up the excess dye. Wash with a solution of washing soda or detergent (not soap) and water. Use a cloth or soft-bristled brush to help scrub. Rinse thoroughly with clear water and allow to dry.

- **Carpet/Wool** • **Silk** • **Wool**

Sponge with water, then apply a Wet Spotter and a few drops of white vinegar. Blot frequently as the stain is loosened. Keep the stain moist with Wet Spotter and vinegar. Flush with water when no more stain is removed. If stain remains, apply rubbing alcohol to the stain and cover with an absorbent pad moistened with alcohol. Let it remain as long as stain is being removed. Change the pad as it picks up the stain. Keep the stain and pad moist with alcohol. Allow to air dry.

- **Cotton** • **Linen**

Soak in a solution of 1 quart warm water, ½ teaspoon dishwashing detergent, and 1 tablespoon ammonia for 30 minutes. Rinse with water. Apply rubbing alcohol and tamp or scrape. Keep the stain moist with alcohol and blot occasionally. Continue as long as stain is being removed. Flush with water and allow to dry. Launder as soon as possible.

- **Grout**

Wipe up excess with a cloth dipped in warm sudsy water. If any stain persists, apply a tile and grout cleaner or dip a wet toothbrush into baking soda or powdered cleanser. Gently scrub the spot. Rinse well and wipe dry.

•Leather •Suede
Dye will immediately change the color of these
materials. Once contact has been made, there
is no way to remove the stain.

•Wood
Mix dishwashing detergent in hot water and
swish to make a great volume of suds. Dip a
cloth in only the foam and apply. Rinse with a
clean cloth moistened with clear water. Polish
or wax as soon as possible.

Dye/Red

**•Acetate •Carpet/Synthetic •Carpet/Wool
•Fiberglass •Rayon •Silk •Triacetate •Wool**
Sponge the area immediately with water to dilute the spill. Carefully use a spot remover.
Apply Wet Spotter and a few drops of ammonia.
(Use ammonia sparingly on silk and wool.)
Cover with an absorbent pad dampened with
the Wet Spotter. Let the pad remain as long as
any stain is being removed. Change the pad as
it picks up the stain. Keep both the stain and
pad moist with Wet Spotter and ammonia. Flush
well with water and repeat if necessary. If, after
allowing to dry, a stain still persists use a commercial color remover according to package direction. After testing on an inconspicuous
place, flush it through the stain to an absorbent
pad. When dealing with carpet, sponge it on the
stain and blot with an absorbent pad. Rinse well
with water and allow to dry thoroughly.

•Acrylic Fabric •Cotton •Linen •Modacrylic •Nylon •Olefin •Polyester •Spandex
Soak the item in a solution of 1 quart warm water, ½ teaspoon liquid dishwashing or laundry detergent, and 1 tablespoon ammonia for 30 minutes. Rinse well. If stain persists, soak in a solution of 1 quart warm water and 1 tablespoon white vinegar for 1 hour. Use white vinegar with care on cotton and linen. Rinse well with water and allow to dry. If stain is set, try applying rubbing alcohol to the area and tamping. As stain loosens, blot liquid and stain with absorbent pad. Keep both the stain and pad moist with alcohol and change pad as it picks up stain. Allow to dry. As a last resort for any remaining traces of stain, mix a commercial color remover according to package direction and apply to stain. After testing on a hidden place, flush the solution through the stain. Rinse well with clear water and allow to dry thoroughly.

•Acrylic Plastic •Aluminum •Bamboo •Cane •Ceramic Glass/Tile •Glass •Paint/Flat •Paint/Gloss •Plexiglas •Polyurethane •Vinyl Clothing •Vinyl Wallcovering
Immediately wipe up the spill with a cloth or sponge dipped in warm sudsy water. Rinse well and wipe dry.

•Alabaster •Marble
Immediately wipe up the spill with a cloth or sponge dipped in warm sudsy water. Rinse well and wipe dry. If a stain persists, soak an absorbent pad in rubbing alcohol, wring dry, and place over the stain. Wait 5 minutes and apply an absorbent pad soaked in ammonia and

wrung out. Alternate the alcohol and ammonia pads until stain has been removed. Wipe surface with cloth dampened with clear water, then wipe dry with clean cloth.

●*Asphalt* ●*Cork* ●*Linoleum* ●*Vinyl Tile*

Wipe up any excess with a cloth or sponge dipped in warm sudsy water. Rinse well and wipe dry. If a stain remains, cover it with an absorbent pad soaked in rubbing alcohol. Let it remain in place for several minutes, then wipe the area with a cloth dampened with ammonia. Do not use ammonia on linoleum or vinyl floor tile. Rinse well with cloth dipped in warm sudsy water and rewipe with a cloth dipped in clear water and squeezed almost dry. Allow to dry.

●*Bluestone* ●*Brick* ●*Concrete* ●*Flagstone* ●*Granite* ●*Limestone* ●*Masonry Tile* ●*Sandstone* ●*Slate* ●*Terrazzo*

Wipe up excess dye. Wash with a solution of washing soda or detergent (not soap) and water. Use a cloth or soft-bristled brush to help scrub. Rinse thoroughly with clear water and allow to dry.

●*Grout*

Wipe up excess with a cloth dipped in warm sudsy water. If any stain persists, dip wet tooth-brush into a little baking soda or powdered cleanser, or apply a tile and grout cleaner and gently scrub the stain. Rinse well with water and wipe dry.

●*Leather* ●*Suede*

Dye will immediately act on the color of the hide. Once contact has been made there is no way to remove the color.

•Wood

Mix dishwashing detergent in hot water and swish to make a great volume of suds. Dip a cloth in only the foam and apply. Rinse with a clean cloth dipped in clear water and wrung out. Polish or wax as soon as possible.

Dye/Yellow

•Acetate •Carpet/Synthetic •Carpet/Wool •Fiberglass •Rayon •Silk •Triacetate •Wool
Sponge the area with dry-cleaning solvent. Then apply a Dry Spotter and tamp or scrape to loosen the stain. Flush with one of the liquid dry-cleaning solvents. If stain persists, apply amyl acetate and tamp again. Flush with the dry-cleaning solvent and allow to dry. If any trace still remains, sponge stain with water and apply a few drops of white vinegar. Tamp or scrape again. Apply a Wet Spotter and a few drops of ammonia, then tamp again. Allow to dry. Sponge with rubbing alcohol and pat with a pad dampened with alcohol—do not use alcohol on acetate, rayon or triacetate. Allow to dry.

•Acrylic Fabric •Cotton •Linen •Modacrylic •Nylon •Olefin •Polyester •Spandex
Cover the stain with a rubbing alcohol compress (dilute alcohol with 2 parts water for acrylic and modacrylic and pretest its effects). Let the compress remain for a few minutes, then wipe stain with a cloth dampened with ammonia. If stain persists, sponge the area with dry-cleaning solvent. Then apply a Dry Spotter. Tamp or scrape

to loosen the stain. Flush with one of the liquid dry-cleaning solvents. If stain persists, apply amyl acetate and tamp again. Flush with the dry-cleaning solvent. If stain still remains, sponge with water and apply a Wet Spotter and a few drops of white vinegar—do not use vinegar on cotton or linen. Tamp again, then apply a Wet Spotter and a few drops of ammonia. Flush with the dry-cleaning solvent and allow to dry.

●Acrylic Plastic ●Aluminum ●Bamboo ●Cane ●Ceramic Glass/Tile ●Glass ●Paint/Flat ●Paint/Gloss ●Plexiglas ●Polyurethane ●Vinyl Clothing ●Vinyl Wallcovering

Immediately wipe up the spill with a cloth or sponge dipped in warm sudsy water. Rinse well and wipe dry.

●Alabaster ●Marble

Immediately wipe up the spill with a cloth or sponge dipped in warm sudsy water. Rinse well and wipe dry. If a stain persists, soak an absorbent pad in rubbing alcohol and place it over the stain. Wait 5 minutes, then apply an absorbent pad soaked with ammonia. Alternate pads until stain has been removed. Rinse surface with cloth dampened with clear water. Wipe dry with clean cloth.

●Asphalt ●Cork ●Linoleum ●Vinyl Tile

Wipe up any excess with a cloth or sponge dipped in warm sudsy water. Rinse well and wipe dry. If stain remains, cover with an absorbent pad soaked in rubbing alcohol. Let it remain in place for several minutes, then wipe the area with a cloth dampened with ammonia. Do not use ammonia on linoleum or vinyl floor tile. Rinse with cloth dipped in warm sudsy water and follow with cloth dampened with clear water. Allow to dry.

●Bluestone ●Brick ●Concrete ●Flagstone ●Granite ●Limestone ●Masonry Tile ●Sandstone ●Slate ●Terrazzo
Wipe up excess dye. Wash with a solution of washing soda or detergent (not soap) and water. Use a cloth or soft-bristled brush to help scrub. Rinse thoroughly with clear water and allow to dry.

●Grout
Wipe up excess spill with a cloth dipped in warm sudsy water. If any stain persists, dip a wet toothbrush into a little baking soda or powdered cleanser, or use a tile and grout cleaner. Gently scrub the stain. Rinse thoroughly and wipe dry.

●Leather ●Suede
Dye will immediately discolor these materials on contact. There is no way to remove this discoloration, as it is absorbed into the hide.

●Wood
Mix dishwashing detergent in hot water and swish to make a great volume of suds. Dip a cloth in only the foam and apply. Rinse with a clean cloth dampened with clear water. Polish or wax as soon as possible.

Eyeliner/Eye Pencil Eyeshadow

●*Acetate* ●*Carpet/Synthetic* ●*Carpet/Wool*
●*Fiberglass* ●*Rayon* ●*Silk* ●*Triacetate* ●*Wool*
Brush or blot up any excess, taking care not to spread the stain. Flush with a dry-cleaning solvent. Apply a Dry Spotter to the stain and cover with an absorbent pad dampened with the Dry Spotter. Check the stain every 5 minutes. Before changing pads, press hard against the stain. Continue the alternate soaking and pressing until no more stain is being removed. Flush with one of the dry-cleaning solvents and allow to dry. If any stain remains, flush it with water and apply a Wet Spotter with a few drops of ammonia. (Do not use ammonia on silk or wool.) Cover with an absorbent pad dampened with the Wet Spotter. Let it stand as long as any stain is being removed. Change the pad as it picks up the stain. Keep the stain and pad moist. Flush well with water. Repeat if necessary; allow to dry.

●*Acrylic Fabric* ●*Cotton* ●*Linen* ●*Modacrylic*
●*Nylon* ●*Olefin* ●*Polyester* ●*Spandex*
Brush or blot away any excess, taking care not to spread the stain. Flush with a dry-cleaning solvent. Apply a Dry Spotter to the stain and cover with a cloth dampened with the Dry Spotter. Check the stain often, tamping before changing the pad. Continue alternate soaking and tamping until no more stain is lifted. Flush with one of the dry-cleaning solvents and allow to dry. If any stain remains, try the same procedure

of soaking and tamping, using a Wet Spotter and a few drops of ammonia. When the stain is gone, be sure to flush the area with water to remove all traces of ammonia. Launder as soon as possible.

•Acrylic Plastic •Alabaster •Asphalt •Bamboo •Cane •Ceramic Glass/Tile •Cork •Enamel •Glass •Gold •Ivory •Jade •Linoleum •Marble •Paint/Flat •Paint/Gloss •Plexiglas •Polyurethane •Stainless Steel •Vinyl Clothing •Vinyl Tile •Vinyl Wallcovering

Wipe any spills or brush away any excess. With a cloth or sponge dipped in warm sudsy water, wash the surface. Rinse well with water and wipe dry with a clean cloth.

•Bluestone •Limestone •Masonry Tile •Sandstone •Slate •Terrazzo

Wipe up excess. Mix solution of washing soda or detergent (not soap) and water. Wash the stained area. Rinse well with clear water and allow to dry.

•Leather •Suede

Gently remove excess. Mix solution of mild soap in lukewarm water. Swish to create a great volume of suds. Apply only the foam with a sponge. Wipe dry with a clean cloth. If a greasy or oily stain remains, powder it with an absorbent such as cornmeal. Give it plenty of time to work. Gently brush or shake the absorbent from the surface. Repeat if necessary. On leather only, follow with saddle soap to condition the leather.

•Wood

Mix dishwashing detergent in hot water and swish to make a great volume of suds. Dip a cloth in only the foam and apply to the stain. Rinse with clear water. Wipe dry immediately with a soft cloth and polish or wax as usual.

Fingernail Polish

●Acetate ●Fiberglass ●Rayon ●Silk ●Triacetate ●Wool

Immediately scrape any excess with a dull knife or spatula. Apply a Dry Spotter to the stain and cover with an absorbent pad dampened with Dry Spotter. Let it stand as long as any stain is being removed. Keep the pad and stain moist. Flush with a dry-cleaning solvent. Allow to dry.

●Acrylic Fabric ●Burlap ●Cotton ●Linen ●Modacrylic ●Nylon ●Olefin ●Polyester ●Rope ●Spandex

Scrape the excess. Test acetone on an inconspicuous place. If fiber color doesn't change, flush acetone through the stain to an absorbent pad. When no more stain is being removed, change pads and flush well with dry-cleaning solvent. Allow to dry thoroughly.

●Acrylic Plastic ●Asphalt ●Cork ●Linoleum ●Plexiglas ●Polyurethane ●Vinyl Clothing ●Vinyl Tile ●Vinyl Wallcovering

Fingernail polish contains chemicals that can quickly ruin the surface. Immediately scrape up any excess spill. Dab the area with a cloth dipped in amyl acetate and rinse, but this stain may be permanent.

●Alabaster ●Marble
Wipe up the excess immediately. Wipe the area with a cloth dampened with acetone. Rinse with a damp cloth and wipe dry. If any stain remains, make a poultice of water, 3% hydrogen peroxide, and a mild powder detergent. Apply the poultice to the stain and cover with a damp cloth. When the stain has been bleached out, rinse thoroughly and dry.

●Aluminum ●Iron ●Stainless Steel ●Tin
Wipe excess immediately. Since these surfaces aren't porous, there shouldn't be a stain, only a mild discoloration. To remove this discoloration, wash with a steel wool soap pad, rinse thoroughly, and dry.

●Bamboo ●Cane
Remove the excess and wipe the area with a cloth dipped in mild pure soapsuds to which a little ammonia has been added. If any stain remains, dip the edge of a clean cloth in acetone and gently dab at the stain—be careful not to force the stain into the plant fibers. If not treated immediately, this could be a permanent stain.

●Bluestone ●Brick ●Concrete ●Flagstone ●Granite ●Limestone ●Masonry Tile ●Sandstone ●Slate ●Terrazzo
Remove the excess as soon as possible. With a cloth dipped in acetone, dab at the remaining stain until no more is picked up. Wash the area using a soft-bristled brush with a solution of washing soda or detergent and water. Rinse with clear water and allow to dry.

•Carpet/Synthetic •Carpet/Wool

Scrape as much of the excess as you can without forcing it into the pile. Apply amyl acetate to the stain and cover with an absorbent pad dampened with amyl acetate. Keep moist and let stand for about 15 minutes, blotting occasionally. Scrape to help loosen the stain. Flush carefully with a dry-cleaning solvent. Allow to thoroughly dry.

•Ceramic Glass/Tile •Enamel •Glass •Gold •Platinum •Porcelain •Rhinestones •Silver

Wipe excess polish as soon as possible. Wash with a cloth dipped in a solution of washing soda, water, and a few drops of ammonia. Rinse well and wipe dry. Hardened polish can sometimes be carefully scraped away with a razor blade on ceramic tile, enamel, and glass.

•Grout

With a sponge, blot up as much polish as possible. Apply a tile and grout cleaner or dip a wet toothbrush into a little powdered cleanser and scrub gently. Rinse well with clear water and wipe dry.

•Jade •Opal •Pearls (except simulated)

Blot excess polish. Fingernail polish may permanently damage natural and cultured pearls and mother-of-pearl. A cotton swab moistened with oily fingernail polish remover (not acetone-based polish remover) and gently dabbed on the stain may be effective. After stained setting has been moistened, blot up stain with a dry cotton swab.

•Leather •Suede

Carefully scrape excess with a dull knife or spatula. Mix a solution of mild soap in lukewarm water. Swish to create a great volume of suds. Appply only the foam with a sponge, but avoid spreading the stain. Dry with a clean cloth. If the polish has hardened, try gently rubbing an artgum eraser across it. As a last resort, cautiously file the area with an emery board or a piece of very fine (grade 6/0—8/0) sandpaper. As a thin layer of hide is removed, work carefully.

•Paint/Flat •Paint/Gloss

Wipe away the excess, being careful not to spread the polish. Wipe the stain with a cloth dipped in 1/3 quart warm sudsy water to which 1 teaspoon borax has been added. Rinse with clear water and dry thoroughly.

Flowers

(Follow procedures for Grass.)

Food Coloring

(See Dye, Dye/Red, Dye/Yellow.)

Fruits

(*See* Berries, Cherry, Grape.)

Grape

•*Acetate* •*Carpet/Synthetic* •*Carpet/Wool*
•*Fiberglass* •*Rayon* •*Rope* •*Triacetate* •*Wool*
Spray on a fabric spot cleaner. If stain remains,
sponge with cool water. Then sponge the area
with lemon juice (or rub the cut sides of a slice
of lemon over the stain). Flush with water. Blot
as much excess liquid as possible and allow to
dry. If stain still persists, apply a Wet Spotter.
Cover with an absorbent pad moistened with
Wet Spotter. Let stand as long as any stain is
being removed. Change the pad as it picks up
the stain. Keep the pad and stained area moist
with Wet Spotter. Flush with water. If any trace
of stain still appears, moisten the area with a
solution of 1 cup warm water and 1 teaspoon
of an enzyme presoak product—do not use on
silk or wool. Cover with clean absorbent pad
that has been dipped in the solution and wrung
almost dry. Let it stand for 30 minutes. Add
enough solution to keep the stain and pad
moist, but do not allow the wet area to spread.
When no more stain is visible, flush thoroughly
with water and allow to air dry.

•*Acrylic Fabric* •*Modacrylic* •*Nylon* •*Olefin*
•*Polyester* •*Spandex*

Spray on a fabric spot cleaner. If stain remains, sponge with cool water immediately. Then sponge with lemon juice or rub a lemon slice over the stain. Flush with water. Blot as much excess liquid as possible and allow to dry. If any trace of stain still exists, presoak in a solution of 1 quart warm water, ½ teaspoon liquid dishwashing or laundry detergent, and 1 tablespoon white vinegar for 15 minutes. Rinse with water and launder if possible. If not, soak in a solution of 1 quart water and 1 tablespoon of an enzyme presoak product for 30 minutes. Rinse well with water and launder as soon as possible.

●*Acrylic Plastic* ●*Aluminum* ●*Asphalt* ●*Bamboo* ●*Brass* ●*Bronze* ●*Cane* ●*Ceramic Glass/Tile* ●*Copper* ●*Enamel* ●*Glass* ●*Grout* ●*Iron* ●*Paint/ Flat* ●*Paint/Gloss* ●*Plexiglas* ●*Polyurethane* ●*Porcelain Dishes* ●*Porcelain Fixtures* ●*Stainless Steel* ●*Vinyl Clothing* ●*Vinyl Wallcovering*
Wipe up any excess spill with cloth or sponge dipped in warm sudsy water. Rinse well and wipe dry.

●*Bluestone* ●*Brick* ●*Concrete* ●*Flagstone* ●*Granite* ●*Masonry Tile* ●*Slate* ●*Terrazzo*
Wipe up excess spill. Wash area with a solution of washing soda or detergent (not soap) and water. Use a soft cloth or soft-bristled brush. Rinse thoroughly with clear water and allow to dry.

●*Cork* ●*Linoleum* ●*Vinyl Tile*
Wipe up excess spill and wash the area with a solution of washing soda or detergent and water. Use a soft-bristled brush or cloth to scrub gently. Rinse thoroughly with clear water and

allow to dry. If stain persists, wipe area with a cloth dampened in a solution of 1 tablespoon oxalic acid and 1 pint water. Rinse well and wipe dry. Repolish the surface if necessary.

●Cotton ●Linen
Test fabric for colorfastness. If color doesn't change, stretch the stain over a bowl; fasten in place with a rubber band. Pour boiling water through the fabric from the height of 2 or 3 feet. Avoid splatters. This procedure must be done immediately. If stain persists, soak in a solution of 1 quart warm water and ½ teaspoon detergent for 15 minutes. Rinse with water. Sponge area with rubbing alcohol and launder if possible. If not, presoak in a solution of 1 quart warm water and 1 tablespoon of an enzyme presoak product for 30 minutes. Rinse well and launder.

●Leather ●Suede
Blot any excess liquid. Mix solution of mild soap in lukewarm water. Swish to create a great volume of suds. Apply only the foam with a sponge. Wipe with a clean dry cloth. On leather only, follow with saddle soap to condition the leather.

●Marble
After wiping up any excess liquid, wipe surface with a cloth or sponge dipped in warm sudsy water. Rinse well and wipe dry. If any stain or discoloration remains, mix a poultice of water, powdered detergent, and chlorine bleach. Apply a thick paste to the stain and cover with a damp cloth to retard evaporation. When the stain has been bleached out, rinse thoroughly and dry.

•Silver
Wash silver as soon as possible in hot sudsy water. Rinse in hot water and dry immediately with a soft cloth to prevent tarnish.

•Wood
Mix dishwashing detergent in hot water and swish to make a great volume of suds. Dip a cloth in only the foam and apply to the grape stain. Rinse with a clean cloth dampened with clear water. If a stain remains, rub the area with a cloth dampened in a solution of 1 tablespoon oxalic acid to 1 pint water. Rinse well and wipe dry. Wax or polish as soon as possible.

Grass

•Acetate •Carpet/Synthetic •Carpet/Wool •Rayon •Silk •Triacetate •Wool
Sponge the area with a dry-cleaning solvent. Apply a Dry Spotter to the stain and cover with an absorbent pad dampened with the Dry Spotter. Let it stand as long as any stain is being removed. Change the pad as it picks up the stain. Keep both the stain and pad moist with Dry Spotter. Flush with dry-cleaning solvent and allow to dry thoroughly. When working on carpets, be sure to blot up the excess liquid during the procedure and before drying.

•Acrylic Fabric •Cotton •Linen •Modacrylic •Nylon •Olefin •Polyester •Spandex
Work liquid dishwashing or laundry detergent

into the stain and rinse well with water. If any stain remains presoak in an enzyme presoak product. Rinse thoroughly and launder as soon as possible. If any stain still remains, test for colorfastness in an inconspicuous place, then use a mild sodium perborate bleach or 3% hydrogen peroxide. Thoroughly rinse with clear water, then launder as usual.

•Acrylic Plastic •Aluminum •Ceramic Glass/ Tile •Cork •Linoleum •Vinyl Clothing •Vinyl Tile •Vinyl Wallcovering
Remove any stains by wiping with a cloth dipped in warm sudsy water. Rinse well and wipe dry with a clean cloth.

•Bluestone •Brick •Concrete •Flagstone •Granite •Limestone •Masonry Tile •Slate •Terrazzo
Wash stain with a solution of washing soda or detergent (not soap) and water. Use a cloth or soft-bristled brush to gently scrub the stain. Rinse thoroughly with clear water and allow to dry.

•Leather •Suede
Mix a solution of mild soap in lukewarm water. Swish to create a great volume of suds. Apply only the foam with a sponge. Wipe with a dry clean cloth. If an oily stain remains, powder the area with an absorbent, such as cornmeal. Allow plenty of time for the absorbent to work, then brush off the stain and powder. Repeat if necessary. On leather only, follow with saddle soap.

Grease
Automotive/Cooking

●*Acetate* ●*Carpet/Synthetic* ●*Carpet/Wool*
●*Rayon* ●*Silk* ●*Triacetate* ●*Wool*
Blot up as much excess as possible and apply
an absorbent, such as cornmeal. After letting
the absorbent work, brush it out of the fabric.
If any stain remains, sponge with a dry-cleaning
solvent. Then apply a Dry Spotter to the area.
Cover the stain wth an absorbent pad dampened
with Dry Spotter. Let it remain in place as long
as any stain is being lifted. Change the pad as
it picks up the stain. Keep both the stain and
pad moist with Dry Spotter. Flush with one of
the dry-cleaning solvents. If a stain still persists, sponge stain with water and apply a Wet
Spotter with a few drops of white vinegar. Cover
the area with an absorbent pad moistened with
Wet Spotter. Let it stand as long as any stain
is being removed. Change the pad as it picks
up the stain. Keep both the stain and pad moist
with Wet Spotter and vinegar. Flush the area
with water and repeat above procedure until no
more stain is removed. Allow to dry.

●*Acrylic Fabric* ●*Cotton* ●*Linen* ●*Modacrylic*
●*Olefin* ●*Polyester* ●*Spandex*
Blot up the excess grease as soon as possible.
Apply an absorbent and let it soak up the spill.
After brushing out the powder, sponge the area

with a dry-cleaning solvent. Then apply a Dry Spotter to any remaining stain. Cover the stain with an absorbent pad dampened with Dry Spotter and let it remain in place until no more stain is lifted. Change the pad as it picks up the stain. To help loosen the stain, occasionally tamp the area, blotting up any loosened material. Flush with one of the liquid dry-cleaning solvents. If any trace of stain remains, sponge stain with water and apply a Wet Spotter and a few drops of ammonia. Tamp the stain again, blotting with an absorbent pad to remove any loosened material. Flush the area with water and repeat until no more stain is removed. Allow to dry.

●*Acrylic Plastic* ●*Aluminum* ●*Asphalt* ●*Bamboo* ●*Cane* ●*Ceramic Glass/Tile* ●*Cork* ●*Glass* ●*Linoleum* ●*Paint/Flat* ●*Paint/Gloss* ●*Pewter* ●*Plexiglas* ●*Polyurethane* ●*Porcelain Dishes* ●*Stainless Steel* ●*Vinyl Clothing* ●*Vinyl Tile* ●*Vinyl Wallcovering*

Blot up any excess grease. Wipe the surface with a cloth or sponge dipped in warm sudsy water. Rinse well and wipe dry.

●*Bluestone* ●*Brick* ●*Concrete* ●*Flagstone* ●*Granite* ●*Limestone* ●*Masonry Tile* ●*Sandstone* ●*Slate* ●*Terrrazzo*

Pour a strong solution of washing soda and boiling water onto the surface. Cover the stain with a paste made of fuller's earth and hot water. Leave overnight. Rinse with clear water. Repeat if necessary.

●*Leather*

Rub the stain with a thick paste of fuller's earth and water. Allow paste to dry, then brush off the powder. Repeat if necessary. Follow with saddle soap to condition the leather.

●*Marble*
Wipe up any excess, then wipe surface with a cloth or sponge dipped in warm sudsy water. Rinse well and wipe dry with a clean cloth. If any residue remains, mix a poultice with water, detergent, and bleach. Apply the poultice to the stain and cover with a dampened cloth to retard evaporation. After the stain has been bleached out, rinse the area thoroughly with water and allow to dry.

●*Suede*
Dip a clean cloth into ground cornmeal and rub in a circular motion into the stain. Gently brush out all the powder with a wire brush. Repeat if necessary. If stain persists, pretest lemon juice in an inconspicuous place, then brush stain with the juice and wire brush. Hold in the steam of a boiling kettle for a few minutes. Brush with a wire brush.

●*Wallpaper*
Make a paste of cornstarch and water. Apply it to the stain and allow to dry. Brush off the powder and repeat if necessary. If the stain persists, make a paste of fuller's earth and trichloroethane. Apply and allow to dry. Brush off.

●*Wood*
Mix dishwashing detergent in hot water and swish to make a great volume of suds. Dip a cloth in only the foam and gently wipe. Rinse with a clean cloth moistened with clear water. Polish or wax as soon as possible.

Ink
Ballpoint, Stamp Pad
(except red)

●*Acetate* ●*Burlap* ●*Carpet/Synthetic* ●*Carpet/ Wool* ●*Fiberglass* ●*Rayon* ●*Silk* ●*Triacetate* ●*Wool*

Sponge the stain with water. Try a light spray of hair spray to loosen the stain, then apply a Wet Spotter and a few drops of white vinegar. Let stand for 30 minutes, blotting every 5 minutes with a clean absorbent pad. Spray on a fabric spot cleaner. Add Wet Spotter and vinegar as needed to keep the stain moist. Flush with water. If stain persists, apply rubbing alcohol to the stain and cover with an absorbent pad moistened with alcohol. Let it stand as long as any stain is being removed. Change the pad as it picks up the stain. Flush with alcohol. (Do not use alcohol on acetate, rayon or triacetate.) If stain traces remain, sponge area with water and apply a Wet Spotter and a few drops of ammonia. Let stand for 30 minutes, blotting every 5 minutes. Add enough Wet Spotter and ammonia (do not use ammonia on silk or wool) to keep the stain moist. Flush with water and allow to dry.

●*Acrylic Fabric* ●*Cotton* ●*Linen* ●*Modacrylic* ●*Nylon* ●*Olefin* ●*Polyester* ●*Spandex*

Try a light spray of hair spray to loosen the stain. Soak in a solution of 1 quart warm water, ½ teaspoon dishwashing detergent, and 1 tablespoon white vinegar for 30 minutes—use care when using vinegar on cotton and linen. Rinse with water and allow to dry. If stain persists, apply rubbing alcohol to the stain and cover with an absorbent pad moistened with alcohol (use alcohol sparingly on acrylic and modacrylic). Let stand as long as any stain is being removed. Change pad as it picks up the stain. Keep both the stain and pad moist with alcohol. Flush with alcohol and allow to dry. If any trace of stain remains, soak in a solution of 1 quart warm water, ½ teaspoon dishwashing detergent, and 1 tablespoon ammonia for 30 minutes. Rinse thoroughly with water and allow to dry.

●Acrylic Plastic ●Ceramic Glass/Tile ●Cork ●Glass ●Plexiglas ●Polyurethane ●Porcelain Fixtures ●Vinyl Clothing ●Vinyl Wallcovering

Apply an all-purpose spray cleaner, following label directions. If any trace of stain remains, cover area with a compress sprinkled with ammonia. Rinse well and wash with a cloth dipped in warm sudsy water. Rinse again and allow to dry.

●Alabaster ●Marble

Wipe the surface with a cloth or sponge dipped in warm sudsy water. Rinse well and wipe dry. If any trace of stain persists, apply an absorbent pad dampened with rubbing alcohol. After several minutes, replace the pad with one moistened with ammonia. Continue alternating alcohol and ammonia treatment until stain is removed. Rinse well and wipe dry.

●Asphalt ●Bluestone ●Brick ●Concrete ●Flagstone ●Sandstone ●Slate ●Terrazzo

Wash with a solution of washing soda or detergent (not soap) and water. Use a cloth or soft-bristled brush to help scrub. Rinse thoroughly with clear water and allow to dry.

●*Bamboo* ●*Cane* ●*Paint/Flat* ●*Paint/Gloss*
Wipe with a cloth dipped in a solution of mild pure soap and water to which a few drops of ammonia have been added. Rinse well and dry thoroughly.

●*Grout*
Wipe stain with a cloth dipped in warm sudsy water. If stain remains, apply a tile and grout cleaner or dip wet toothbrush into a little baking soda or powdered cleanser and gently scrub. Rinse well and wipe dry.

●*Leather* ●*Suede*
On leather or suede, apply a cleaner for that surface. Rub it in with a clean soft cloth and let it dry. If any stain still remains, try gingerly applying a dry-cleaning solvent. Dab it on with a clean cloth, after testing on a hidden seam. Allow to air dry. On leather only, follow with saddle soap to condition the leather. **Caution:** There is no guaranteed way to remove this stain from these materials.

●*Linoleum* ●*Vinyl Tile*
First, apply an all-purpose spray cleaner according to package directions. If any stain remains, cover the area with a compress made with rubbing alcohol. Rinse with clear water. If stain persists, rub the area with superfine (number 0000) steel wool dipped in liquid floor wax. Wash the area with soapy water, dry, then wax as usual.

●*Wallpaper*

Try removing any ink with a soft eraser. Work in small movements to avoid tearing the paper. If the stain persists, wipe the area with a cloth or sponge moistened with cool clear water. Overlap the strokes to avoid streaking. Use a clean cloth to gently pat dry.

●*Wood*

Mix dishwashing detergent in hot water and swish to make a great volume of suds. Dip a cloth in only the foam and gently wipe the stain. Rinse with a clean cloth moistened with clear water. If a stain remains, rub the area with superfine (number 0000) steel wool dipped in liquid wax. Rub lightly, because steel wool will remove a fine layer of the surface. Polish or wax as soon as possible.

Ink/Ballpoint, Stamp Pad (Red)

●*Acetate* ●*Carpet/Synthetic* ●*Carpet/Wool* ●*Fiberglass* ●*Rayon* ●*Silk* ●*Triacetate* ●*Wool*

Sponge the area immediately with water to dilute the ink. Spraying on a fabric spot cleaner may help to remove the ink. Apply a Wet Spotter and a few drops of ammonia. (Use ammonia with care on silk and wool.) Cover with an absorbent pad dampened with the Wet Spotter. Let the pad remain as long as any stain is being removed. Change the pad as it picks up the stain. Flush well with water and repeat if necessary. If after drying, a stain persists, mix a commercial color remover according to package directions. After testing on a hidden seam, flush it through the stain to an absorbent pad beneath. When dealing with carpeting, sponge the color remover on the stain and blot with an absorbent pad. Rinse well with water and allow to dry thoroughly.

●*Acrylic Fabric* ●*Cotton* ●*Linen* ●*Modacrylic* ●*Nylon* ●*Olefin* ●*Polyester* ●*Spandex*

Soak the item in a solution of 1 quart warm water, ½ teaspoon dishwashing detergent, and 1 tablespoon ammonia for 30 minutes. Rinse well. If stain remains, soak in a solution of 1 quart warm water and 1 tablespoon white vinegar for 1 hour. (Take care when using vinegar on cotton and linen.) Rinse well and allow to dry. If stain has set, apply rubbing alcohol to the area (dilute with 2 parts water for acrylic or modacrylic) and tamp. As stain loosens, blot liquid and stain with an absorbent pad. Keep both the stain and pad moist with alcohol and change pad as it picks up the stain. Allow to dry. As a last resort for any remaining stain, pretest a color remover in an inconspicuous place, then apply to the stain. Flush the solution through the stain and into an absorbent pad beneath. Rinse well with clear water and allow to dry.

●*Acrylic Plastic* ●*Aluminum* ●*Bamboo* ●*Cane* ●*Ceramic Glass/Tile* ●*Paint/Flat* ●*Paint/Gloss* ●*Plexiglas* ●*Polyurethane* ●*Vinyl Clothing* ●*Vinyl Wallcovering*

Immediately wipe up the spill with a cloth or sponge dipped in warm sudsy water. Rinse well and wipe dry.

•Alabaster •Marble

Immediately wipe up the spill with a cloth or sponge dipped in warm sudsy water. Rinse well and wipe dry. If a stain remains, soak an absorbent pad in rubbing alcohol, wring almost dry, and place over the stain. Wait 5 minutes and apply an absorbent pad soaked with ammonia and squeezed until damp. Alternate pads until stain has been removed. Wipe surface with cloth moistened with clear water and wipe dry with a clean cloth.

•Asphalt •Cork •Linoleum •Vinyl Tile

Wipe up any excess ink with a cloth or sponge dipped in warm sudsy water. Rinse well and wipe dry. If a stain remains, cover the stain with an absorbent pad soaked in rubbing alcohol. Let it remain in place for several minutes, then wipe the area with a cloth dampened with ammonia. (Do not use ammonia on linoleum or vinyl floor tile.) Rinse well with a cloth dipped in warm sudsy water. Wipe with a cloth moistened with clear water and allow to dry.

•Bluestone •Brick •Concrete •Flagstone •Granite •Masonry Tile •Sandstone •Slate •Terrazzo

Wipe up the excess. Wash with a solution of washing soda or detergent (not soap) and water. Use a cloth or soft-bristled brush to help scrub. Rinse thoroughly with clear water and allow to dry.

•Grout

Wipe up excess with a cloth dipped in warm sudsy water. If any stain remains, apply a tile and grout cleaner or dip a wet toothbrush into baking soda or powdered cleanser and gently scrub the stain. Rinse well with water and wipe dry.

●*Leather* ●*Suede*

Ink spilled on these materials will act immediately on the hide. Once contact has been made, it is impossible to remove.

●*Wood*

Mix dishwashing detergent in hot water and swish to make a great volume of suds. Dip a cloth in only the foam and gently wipe up the ink. Rinse with a clean cloth moistened with clear water. Polish or wax as soon as possible.

Ink/Felt Tip, India

●*Acetate* ●*Burlap* ●*Fiberglass* ●*Rayon* ●*Rope* ●*Silk* ●*Triacetate* ●*Wool*

Sponge the area with a dry-cleaning solvent, then apply a Dry Spotter to the stain. Cover with an absorbent pad moistened with Dry Spotter. Be sure to keep the stain from bleeding. Change the pad as it picks up the stain. Keep the stain and pad moist with Dry Spotter. Flush with a liquid dry-cleaning solvent. If stain persists, sponge with water and apply a Wet Spotter and a few drops of ammonia. (Do not use ammonia on silk or wool.) Cover the stain with an absorbent pad moistened with Wet Spotter. Change the pad as it picks up the stain. Keep both the pad and stain moist with Wet Spotter and white vinegar. Flush with water and repeat as necessary. Allow to dry. Note: Permanent inks are almost impossible to remove.

●Acrylic Fabric ●Cotton ●Linen ●Modacrylic
Sponge the area with a dry-cleaning solvent. If stain remains, mix a paste of powdered detergent, water, and a few drops of ammonia. Apply to the stain. Place an absorbent pad under the stain. When no more stain is being removed, flush thoroughly with water and launder. Note: Permanent inks are almost impossible to remove.

●Acrylic Plastic ●Aluminum ●Asphalt ●Bamboo ●Cane ●Ceramic Glass/Tile ●Enamel ●Glass ●Paint/Flat ●Paint/Gloss ●Plexiglas ●Polyurethane ●Porcelain Dishes ●Porcelain Fixtures ●Stainless Steel ●Vinyl Clothing ●Vinyl Wallcovering
Wipe the surface with a cloth or sponge dipped in warm sudsy water to which a few drops of ammonia have been added. Rinse well with clear water and wipe dry. Note: Permanent inks are almost impossible to remove.

●Alabaster ●Marble
Wipe surface with a cloth or sponge dipped in warm sudsy water to which a few drops of ammonia have been added. Rinse well and wipe dry. If stain persists, apply a cloth soaked in rubbing alcohol; allow it to stand for 15 minutes. Next, apply a cloth soaked with ammonia for 15 minutes. Alternate alcohol and ammonia applications until stain is removed. Rinse thoroughly and wipe dry.

●*Bluestone* ●*Brick* ●*Concrete* ●*Flagstone*
●*Granite* ●*Limestone* ●*Masonry Tile*
●*Sandstone* ●*Slate* ●*Terrazzo*

Wash stain with a solution of washing soda or detergent (never soap) and water. Use a cloth or soft-bristled brush to help scrub. Rinse thoroughly with clear water and allow to dry.

●*Carpet/Synthetic* ●*Carpet/Wool*

Blot as much stain as possible without forcing it deeper into the pile. Sponge the stain with a concentrated solution of carpet spotter.
Caution: Never rub ink stains on carpet. Continue to sponge the area, rinsing the sponge as it picks up the stain. Repeat until no more stain is removed. If the stain persists, have the rug professionally cleaned. Repeated applications of a liquid all-purpose cleaner solution also will help remove the ink. Note: Permanent inks are almost impossible to remove.

●*Cork* ●*Linoleum* ●*Vinyl Tile*

Cover the stain with a compress made with rubbing alcohol. Let the compress remain in place for 5 minutes. Wipe the area with a cloth dampened with ammonia. Do not use ammonia on linoleum or vinyl tile. Rinse well with water and allow to dry. Note: Permanent inks are almost impossible to remove.

●*Felt* ●*Fur/Natural* ●*Fur/Synthetic* ●*Leather*
●*Suede*

Due to the nature of the material involved, this stain can only be removed professionally.

●*Grout*

Wipe stain with cloth dipped in warm sudsy water. If stain remains, apply a tile and grout cleaner or dip a wet toothbrush into a little baking soda or powdered cleanser. Gently scrub the spot. Rinse and wipe dry.

●*Nylon* ●*Olefin* ●*Polyester* ●*Spandex*
Sponge stain with detergent solution immediately. Then apply a dry cleaning solvent. Sprinkle lemon juice and salt over the stain and leave for 1 hour. Rinse well, repeat if necessary, and launder as soon as possible.

●*Wallpaper*
Try erasing light marks with an art gum eraser. If stain remains, rub area lightly with a dry steel wool soap pad. If the stain persists, rub very gently with baking soda sprinkled on a damp cloth. Then wipe the area with a cloth or sponge moistened in cool clear water. Overlap strokes to prevent streaking. Use a clean pad to gently pat dry.

●*Wood*
Dilute oxalic acid in warm water and apply with an artist's brush to the stained area. **Caution:** Oxalic acid is poisonous, so wear rubber gloves when applying it. On painted surfaces, wipe with a cloth moistened with detergent suds. For unpainted or stripped surfaces, after applying the oxalic acid, neutralize the area with white vinegar and rinse with rubbing alcohol. Allow to dry. Note: Permanent inks are almost impossible to remove.

Lipstick

*•Acetate •Carpet/Synthetic •Carpet/Wool
•Fiberglass •Modacrylic •Rayon •Silk
•Triacetate •Wool*

Sponge the area with a dry-cleaning solvent.
Then apply a Dry Spotter and blot immediately
with an absorbent pad. Continue sponging and
blotting until no more stain is removed. If stain
begins to spread, flush immediately with one of
the liquid dry-cleaning solvents. Let all the solvent evaporate, then sponge the area with water.
Apply Wet Spotter and a few drops of ammonia
(do not use ammonia on silk or wool). Blot frequently with an absorbent pad. Flush with water
to remove all ammonia. Apply Wet Spotter and
a few drops of white vinegar. Blot frequently
with an absorbent pad. Flush with water and
allow to dry.

*•Acrylic Fabric •Cotton •Linen •Nylon •Olefin
•Polyester •Spandex*

Pretreat with a laundry prewash product as directed and rinse in warm water. If color remains,
presoak in 1 quart warm water and 1 tablespoon
of an enzyme presoak product for 1 hour. Launder immediately, if possible. If not, rinse well
and dry thoroughly. If any stain remains, apply
a dry-cleaning solvent and Dry Spotter. Blot immediately with an absorbent pad. If stain begins
to spread, flush immediately with one of the
liquid dry-cleaning solvents. Let all the solvent
evaporate. If solvent still remains, sponge with
water and apply a Wet Spotter with a few drops
of ammonia. Tamp and blot frequently with an

absorbent pad. Flush well with water. Allow to dry. Launder as soon as possible.

●Acrylic Plastic ●Ceramic Glass/Tile ●Glass ●Paint/Flat ●Paint/Gloss ●Plexiglas ●Polyurethane ●Porcelain Dishes ●Porcelain Fixtures ●Stainless Steel ●Vinyl Clothing ●Vinyl Wallcovering
Wipe stain with a cloth dipped in warm sudsy water. Rinse well and wipe dry. If stain remains, add a few drops of ammonia to warm sudsy water and wipe. Rinse well, then dry with a clean cloth.

●Alabaster ●Marble
Mix a few drops of ammonia in 1 cup rubbing alcohol. Soak a white blotter with the solution and place it over the stain. Weight it down with a piece of glass or other heavy object. Continue applying the solution until the grease is drawn out and any remaining stain is bleached out. If any color remains, make a poultice of bleach, powdered detergent, and water. Apply to the stain and cover with a damp cloth to retard drying. Leave until stain has been bleached out.

●Asphalt ●Cork ●Linoleum ●Vinyl Tile
Mix a solution of warm sudsy water and a few drops of ammonia. Dip a plastic scouring pad (do not use steel wool) into the solution and rub gently. Rinse well and wipe dry.

●Fur/Natural ●Fur/Synthetic ●Leather ●Suede
Gently scrape to remove excess lipstick. Wipe stain with a cloth dipped in the suds of a mild detergent and water. Wipe with a clean dry cloth. If a grease stain remains, powder the stain with

an absorbent such as cornmeal. Give it plenty of time to work. Gently brush it out. Repeat if necessary. As a last resort, dip a cloth in a dry cleaning solvent and dab gently at stain. Do not rub. On leather only, follow with saddle soap to condition the leather.

Mustard

●*Acetate* ●*Burlap* ●*Carpet/Synthetic* ●*Carpet/Wool* ●*Fiberglass* ●*Rayon* ●*Silk* ●*Triacetate* ●*Wool*

Note: Mustard contains turmeric, a yellow dye. If not treated immediately, it can be impossible to remove. Lift off any excess spill with a dull knife or spatula. Flush the area with a dry-cleaning solvent. If fabric is strong enough, tamp or scrape to loosen the stain. Flush with the dry-cleaning solvent. While tamping stain, blot excess material with an absorbent pad. If stain remains, sponge with water and apply a Wet Spotter and a few drops of white vinegar. Tamp again to loosen stain. Flush with water. If stain persists, moisten area with 3% hydrogen peroxide and add a drop of ammonia (except on silk and wool). Do not let it bleach any longer than 15 minutes, then flush with water and allow to dry. When treating carpets, blot all excess liquid, then weight down an absorbent pad with a heavy object. When all liquid has been absorbed, allow to thoroughly air dry.

●*Acrylic Fabric* ●*Cotton* ●*Linen* ●*Modacrylic* ●*Nylon* ●*Olefin* ●*Polyester* ●*Spandex*

Note: Mustard contains turmeric, a yellow dye. If not treated immediately, it can be impossible to remove. If stain has just occurred, spray on a fabric spot remover. Or, if stain is older, scrape as much of the spill as possible. Flush with water, apply liquid detergent to the stain, and flush again. If the stain remains, presoak for several hours or overnight in a warm-to-hot solution of detergent. Rinse and launder as soon as possible.

●*Acrylic Plastic* ●*Asphalt* ●*Vinyl Clothing* ●*Vinyl Tile* ●*Vinyl Wallcovering*
Note: Mustard contains turmeric, a yellow dye. If not treated immediately, it can be impossible to remove. Once mustard has set, the stain is almost impossible to remove from plastic materials. Immediately wipe up any spills with a cloth or sponge dipped in warm sudsy water. Rinse thoroughly and wipe dry with a soft cloth.

●*Aluminum* ●*Bamboo* ●*Cane* ●*Ceramic Glass/ Tile* ●*Cork* ●*Glass* ●*Linoleum* ●*Paint/Flat* ●*Paint/Gloss* ●*Plexiglas* ●*Polyurethane* ●*Porcelain Dishes* ●*Stainless Steel* ●*Tin* ●*Zinc*
Scrape to remove any excess spill (except on ceramic glass rangetops). Wipe the area with a cloth or sponge dipped in warm sudsy water. Rinse well with water and wipe dry with a soft cloth.

●*Bluestone* ●*Brick* ●*Concrete* ●*Flagstone* ●*Granite* ●*Limestone* ●*Masonry Tile* ●*Sandstone* ●*Slate* ●*Terrazzo*
Remove any excess spill. Wash stain with a solution of washing soda and water. Use a cloth or soft-bristled brush to help clean. Rinse thoroughly with clear water and allow to air dry.

•Grout

Wipe up any excess with a cloth dipped in warm sudsy water. If any stain remains, apply a tile and grout cleaner or dip a wet toothbrush into a little baking soda or powdered cleanser and gently scrub the spot. Rinse thoroughly and wipe dry with a soft cloth.

•Leather •Suede

Note: Mustard contains turmeric, a yellow dye. If not treated immediately, it can be impossible to remove. Although mustard usually causes permanent stains on these materials, try mixing a solution of mild soap in lukewarm water, swishing to create a great volume of suds, and applying only the foam with a sponge. Wipe with a clean cloth dampened with clear water. Dry with a soft cloth. On leather only, follow with saddle soap to condition the leather.

•Silver

Wash in hot soapy water as soon as possible. Rinse in hot water and dry with a soft cloth immediately.

•Wallpaper

The turmeric in mustard usually stains wallpaper permanently. If the stain is fresh, gently wipe the stain with a cloth dipped in the suds of a mild detergent and water. Rinse with a clean cloth moistened with cool clear water. Gently pat dry.

•Wood

Immediately mix dishwashing detergent in hot water and swish to make a great volume of suds. Dip a cloth in only the foam and apply to the mustard. Rinse with a clean cloth dampened with cool clear water. Polish or wax when dry.

Oil/Automotive, Hair, Lubricating, Mineral, Vegetable

●*Acetate* ●*Carpet/Synthetic* ●*Carpet/Wool*
●*Rayon* ●*Silk* ●*Triacetate* ●*Wool*

Blot up as much excess as possible and apply an absorbent such as cornmeal. After letting the absorbent work, brush the powder off the fabric. If a stain remains, sponge with a dry-cleaning solvent. Apply a Dry Spotter. Cover with an absorbent pad that has been dampened with Dry Spotter. Let it remain in place as long as any stain is being removed. Change the pad as it picks up the stain. Keep both the stain and pad moist with Dry Spotter. Flush the area with the dry-cleaning solvent. If a stain persists, sponge the area with water and apply a Wet Spotter with a few drops of white vinegar. Cover the stain with an absorbent pad moistened with Wet Spotter. Let the pad stay in place as long as any stain is being removed. Change the pad as it picks up the stain. Keep both the stain and pad moist with Wet Spotter and vinegar. Flush with water and repeat the procedure until no more stain is removed. Allow to dry.

●*Acrylic Fabric* ●*Cotton* ●*Linen* ●*Modacrylic*
●*Nylon* ●*Olefin* ●*Polyester* ●*Spandex*

Blot excess spill as soon as possible. Apply an absorbent and allow it to soak up remaining spill. After brushing out the powder, sponge the area with a dry-cleaning solvent. Apply a Dry Spotter and cover with an absorbent pad moistened with Dry Spotter. Let it remain in place until no more stain is removed. Change the pad as it picks up the stain. To help loosen the stain, occasionally tamp the area, blotting any loosened material. Flush with one of the liquid dry-cleaning solvents. If any trace of the stain remains, sponge the stain with water and apply a Wet Spotter and a few drops of ammonia. Tamp the stain again, blotting with an absorbent pad. Flush the area with water and repeat until no more stain is removed. Allow to dry.

●*Acrylic Plastic* ●*Aluminum* ●*Asphalt* ●*Bamboo* ●*Cane* ●*Ceramic /Tile* ●*Cork* ●*Glass* ●*Linoleum* ●*Paint/Gloss* ●*Pewter* ●*Plexiglas* ●*Polyurethane* ●*Porcelain Dishes* ●*Stainless Steel* ●*Vinyl Clothing* ●*Vinyl Tile* ●*Vinyl Wallcovering*
Blot up any excess spill. Wipe the surface with a cloth or sponge dipped in warm sudsy water. Rinse well and wipe thoroughly dry.

●*Bluestone* ●*Brick* ●*Concrete* ●*Flagstone* ●*Granite* ●*Limestone* ●*Masonry Tile* ●*Sandstone* ●*Slate* ●*Terrazzo*
Wash with a strong solution of washing soda and hot water. If stain remains, make a paste of 1 pound strong powdered cleaner, 2 cups powdered chalk, and 1 gallon water and cover the stain. Or, cover with a paste made from fuller's earth and hot water. Leave the paste on overnight. Rinse with clear water. Repeat if necessary.

●Leather

Rub a stain with a thick paste of fuller's earth and water. Allow it to dry, then brush off the powder. Condition leather with saddle soap.

●Marble

Remove any excess, then wipe with a cloth dipped in warm sudsy water. Rinse well and wipe dry with a clean cloth. If any residue remains, mix a poultice of water, powdered detergent, and bleach. Apply to the stain and cover with a dampened cloth to retard evaporation. After the stain has been bleached out and the oil removed, rinse thoroughly with water and allow to dry.

●Paint/Flat ●Wallpaper

Make a paste of cornstarch and water. Apply to the stain and allow to dry. Brush off the powder and repeat if necessary. If the stain persists, make a paste of fuller's earth and trichloroethane. **Caution:** Use trichloroethane with care and wear rubber gloves. Apply to stain and allow to dry. Brush off.

●Silver

Immediately wash in hot soapy water. Rinse thoroughly in hot water and dry with a soft clean cloth.

●Suede

Test any treatment in an inconspicuous place first. Dip a clean cloth into ground cornmeal and rub into the stain with a circular motion. Gently brush out the powder with a wire brush. Repeat if necessary. If stain persists, brush stain with lemon juice and hold in steam of a boiling teakettle for a few minutes. Brush with a wire brush.

•Wood
Mix dishwashing detergent in hot water and swish to make a great volume of suds. Dip a cloth in only the foam and apply to the stain. Rinse with a clean cloth dampened with clear water. Polish or wax as soon as possible.

Perspiration

•Acetate •Rayon •Silk •Wool
Sponge the area with water, then spray on a fabric spot cleaner. Follow with an application of Wet Spotter and a few drops of ammonia. (Take care when using ammonia on silk and wool.) Cover with an absorbent pad moistened with Wet Spotter. Let the pad remain in place as long as any stain is being removed. Change the pad as it picks up the stain. Keep both the stain and pad moist with Wet Spotter and ammonia. Flush well with water and allow to dry thoroughly.

•Acrylic Fabric •Cotton •Linen •Modacrylic •Nylon •Olefin •Polyester •Spandex
Presoak the stained garment in an enzyme presoak product according to package directions. After soaking, launder as usual. For older stains, sponge area with a diluted solution of white vinegar and water, then launder. If fabric color has changed, stretch the stained area over a bowl of ammonia so fumes penetrate while

the spot is moist. Prompt treatment of perspiration stains is necessary, as they can weaken most fibers. **Caution:** Never iron a garment with perspiration stains—the heat will set them.

●*Leather* ●*Suede*
Mix a solution of mild soap in lukewarm water. Swish to create a great volume of suds. Apply only the foam with a sponge. Wipe with a clean dry cloth. On leather only, follow with saddle soap to condition the leather.

●*Vinyl Clothing*
Wipe the stain with a cloth dipped in warm sudsy water to which a few drops of ammonia have been added. Rinse well and wipe dry with a clean cloth.

Rust

●*Acetate* ●*Fiberglass* ●*Rayon* ●*Silk* ●*Triacetate* ●*Wool*
Because of the degree of difficulty involved in the removal of rust stains, it is best not to try removing this from these delicate fabrics yourself.

●*Acrylic Fabric* ●*Modacrylic* ●*Nylon* ●*Olefin* ●*Polyester*
Apply lemon juice to the stain, but do not let it dry. Rinse thoroughly with water. If possible, launder. If not and the stain remains, test a fabric-safe rust remover, then apply according to package directions. After using, flush the area with cool water and launder as soon as

possible. **Caution:** Be careful not to spill
rust remover on porcelain or enamel finishes
(like those on washing machines), as
these products can ruin the finish.

●*Asphalt* ●*Linoleum* ●*Vinyl Tile*

Wipe the stain with a cloth or sponge dipped
in warm sudsy water. Rinse well and wipe dry.
If any stain remains, use a rust remover which
is safe for resilient floors.

●*Brick* ●*Concrete* ●*Granite*

Make a poultice from 7 parts lime-free glycerine,
1 part sodium citrate (available from drug
stores), 6 parts lukewarm water, and enough
powdered calcium carbonate (chalk) to create a
thick paste. Apply this paste to the stain and
allow to harden. Remove with a wooden scraper
and repeat if necessary. Wash area thoroughly
with clear water and let dry.

●*Carpet/Synthetic* ●*Carpet/Wool*

Apply lemon juice and salt to the stain. Flush
with water and blot well. If any stain remains,
test a fabric-safe rust remover; if the fabric is
not damaged, apply according to label directions. Flush thoroughly with water; blot excess
liquid. Allow to dry.

●*Ceramic Tile* ●*Porcelain Dishes*
●*Porcelain Fixtures*

On the tub, sink, ceramic tile, or toilet, wet a
pumice bar, and rub the iron stain.
Caution: Do not use pumice on the ceramic
glass found on cookware or ceramic cooktops,
as it will scratch the surface. A paste of borax
and lemon juice also is effective on iron stains.
Rub the paste into the stain and allow it to dry.

Rinse with clear water, then repeat if necessary. Rinse again and dry with a clean cloth.

●Cotton ●Linen

Rub liquid dishwashing or laundry detergent into the stain, rinse with water, and launder as soon as possible. If stain remains, test fabric for colorfastness, then use a fabric-safe rust remover according to package directions.

●Leather ●Suede

Iron and rust are chemical stains that should be treated by a professional cleaner.

●Stainless Steel

Rub stainless steel with a damp piece of very fine grade emery paper, followed by rubbing it with a slice of onion. Rinse well with hot water and dry thoroughly with a soft cloth.

Tomato/Tomato Juice/ Tomato Sauce

●Acetate ●Carpet/Synthetic ●Carpet/Wool ●Fiberglass ●Rayon ●Rope ●Silk ●Triacetate ●Wool

Sponge the stain with cool water, then sponge the area with lemon juice or rub a slice of lemon over the stain (use with caution on wool). Flush with water and blot as much liquid as possible. Let dry. If stain persists, apply a Wet Spotter and cover with an absorbent pad moistened with Wet Spotter. Let stand as long as any stain is being removed. Change the pad as it picks up the stain. Keep the stain and pad moist with Wet Spotter. Flush with water. If any trace of the stain remains, moisten the area with a solution of 1 cup warm water and 1 teaspoon of an enzyme presoak product—do not use on silk or wool. Cover with a clean pad dampened with the solution and wrung almost dry. Let it stand for 30 minutes. Add enough solution to keep the stain and pad moist and warm, but do not allow the wet area to spread. When no more stain is visible, flush thoroughly with water and allow to air dry.

●*Acrylic Fabric* ●*Modacrylic* ●*Nylon* ●*Olefin*
●*Polyester* ●*Spandex*
Sponge stain with cool water immediately. Then rub with a lemon slice or sponge lemon juice on the stain. Flush with water, blotting as much liquid as possible. Allow to dry. If any trace of stain persists, presoak in a solution of 1 quart warm water, ½ teaspoon dishwashing detergent, and 1 tablespoon white vinegar for 15 minutes. Rinse with water and launder if possible. If not, presoak in a solution of 1 quart warm water and 1 tablespoon of an enzyme presoak product. Rinse well with water and launder as soon as possible.

●*Acrylic Plastic* ●*Aluminum* ●*Asphalt* ●*Bamboo*
●*Brass* ●*Bronze* ●*Cane* ●*Ceramic Glass/Tile*
●*Copper* ●*Enamel* ●*Glass* ●*Grout* ●*Iron* ●*Paint/*
Flat ●*Paint/Gloss* ●*Plexiglas* ●*Polyurethane*
●*Porcelain Dishes*
●*Porcelain Fixtures* ●*Stainless Steel*
●*Vinyl Clothing* ●*Vinyl Wallcovering*
Wipe the stain with a cloth or sponge dipped in warm sudsy water. Rinse well and wipe dry.

●Bluestone ●Brick ●Concrete ●Flagstone ●Granite ●Masonry Tile ●Slate ●Terrazzo

Wipe up excess spill and wash the stain with a solution of washing soda or detergent (not soap) and water. Use a cloth or soft-bristled brush to scrub. Rinse thoroughly and allow to dry.

●Cork ●Linoleum ●Vinyl Tile

Wipe up the excess spill and wash the area with a solution of washing soda or detergent (not soap) and water. Scrub with a cloth or soft-bristled brush. Rinse thoroughly with clear water and allow to dry. If stain persists, wipe area with a cloth dampened in a solution of 1 tablespoon oxalic acid to 1 pint water. Rinse well and wipe dry. Repolish the surface if needed.
Caution: Oxalic acid is poisonous; use with care and wear rubber gloves.

●Cotton ●Linen

Test fabric for colorfastness. If colorfast, stretch the stained fabric over a bowl and fasten in place with a rubber band. Pour boiling water through the fabric from a height of 2 or 3 feet. Avoid splatters. This procedure must be done immediately. If stain persists, soak in a solution of 1 quart warm water and ½ teaspoon detergent for 15 minutes. Rinse with water. Sponge area with rubbing alcohol and launder if possible. If not, presoak for 30 minutes in a solution of 1 quart warm water and 1 tablespoon of an enzyme presoak product. Rinse well with water and launder.

●Leather ●Suede

Wipe up any excess juice, then mix a solution of mild soap in lukewarm water. Swish to create a great volume of suds. Apply only the foam with a sponge. Wipe with a clean dry cloth. On leather only, follow with saddle soap to condition the leather.

●Marble
After removing any excess liquid, wipe the surface with a cloth dipped in warm sudsy water. Rinse well and wipe dry. If any stain or discoloration remains, mix a poultice of water, powdered detergent, and bleach. Apply a thick paste to the stain and cover with a damp cloth to retard evaporation. Leave in place. When stain has been removed, rinse thoroughly with water and dry.

●Silver
Wash silver in hot sudsy water as soon as possible. Rinse in hot water and dry immediately with a soft cloth to prevent tarnish.

●Wood
Mix dishwashing detergent in hot water and swish to make a great volume of suds. Dip a cloth in only the foam and apply to the tomato stain. Rinse with a clean cloth moistened with clear water. If any stain remains, rub the area with a cloth dampened with a solution of 1 tablespoon oxalic acid and 1 pint water. Rinse well and wipe dry. Wax or polish as soon as possible. **Caution:** Oxalic acid is poisonous; use with care and wear rubber gloves.

Vegetables/Green, Yellow

●*Acetate* ●*Carpet/Synthetic* ●*Carpet/Wool*
●*Fiberglass* ●*Rayon* ●*Silk* ●*Triacetate* ●*Wool*
Scrape to remove any excess. Sponge the area
with a dry-cleaning solvent. Apply a Dry Spotter
and cover with an absorbent pad moistened with
Dry Spotter. Let it stand as long as any stain
is being removed. Change the pad as it picks
up the stain. Keep the stain and pad moist with
Dry Spotter. Flush with one of the liquid dry-
cleaning solvents. If any stain remains, moisten
the area with a solution of 1 teaspoon enzyme
presoak and 1 cup warm water—do not use enzyme presoaks on silk or wool. Cover the stain
with a pad that has been dipped in the solution
and wrung nearly dry. Let it stand for 30 minutes. Add enough solution to keep the area
warm and barely moist. When no more stain is
being lifted, flush with water and allow to dry.

●*Acrylic Fabric* ●*Cotton* ●*Linen* ●*Modacrylic*
●*Nylon* ●*Olefin* ●*Polyester* ●*Spandex*
Scrape to remove the material. Sponge the area
with a dry-cleaning solvent. Apply a Dry Spotter
and cover with an absorbent pad dampened with
the Dry Spotter. Let it stand as long as any stain
is being removed. Flush with one of the liquid
dry-cleaning solvents. If any stain remains,

apply a few drops of dishwashing detergent and a few drops of ammonia to the area. Tamp or scrape to help loosen the stain. Keep the stain moist with detergent and ammonia and blot occasionally with an absorbent pad. Flush well with water and allow to dry. Launder as soon as possible.

•*Acrylic Plastic* •*Aluminum* •*Asphalt* •*Bamboo* •*Cane* •*Ceramic Glass/Tile* •*Chromium* •*Copper* •*Cork* •*Glass* •*Linoleum* •*Marble* •*Paint/Flat* •*Paint/Gloss* •*Plexiglas* •*Polyurethane* •*Porcelain* •*Stainless Steel* •*Vinyl Clothing* •*Vinyl Tile* •*Vinyl Wallcovering*
Note: If not removed immediately, action of vegetables causes "green rust" on uncoated copper. Wipe up any excess material immediately. Wipe the surface with a cloth or sponge dipped in warm sudsy water. Rinse well and wipe dry with a soft cloth.

•*Bluestone* •*Brick* •*Concrete* •*Flagstone* •*Granite* •*Limestone* •*Masonry Tile* •*Sandstone* •*Slate* •*Terrazzo*
Wipe up any excess vegetable. Wash the surface with a solution of washing soda or detergent (never soap) and water. Use a sponge or soft-bristled brush to scrub. Rinse thoroughly with water and allow to dry.

•*Leather* •*Suede*
Carefully wipe or scrape to remove the excess spill. Mix a solution of mild soap in lukewarm water. Swish to create a great volume of suds. Apply only the foam with a sponge. Wipe dry with a clean cloth. If a greasy stain remains, apply an absorbent such as cornmeal. Give it

plenty of time to work. Gently brush it off. Repeat if necessary. On leather only, follow with saddle soap to condition the leather.

●*Wood*
Wipe up any excess material. Wipe the stain with a cloth dipped in warm sudsy water. Rinse with a clean cloth dampened with clear water. Polish or wax as soon as possible after drying.

Wine/Red, Rose

●*Acetate* ●*Fiberglass* ●*Rayon* ●*Triacetate*
Blot up the excess with a clean cloth. Spray on a fabric spot cleaner. Sponge any remaining stain with water and apply a Wet Spotter and a few drops of white vinegar. Cover with an absorbent pad moistened with Wet Spotter. Let it remain as long as any stain is being removed. Change the pad as it picks up the stain. Keep the stain and pad moist with Wet Spotter and vinegar. Flush with water. Repeat until no more stain is removed. If a stain remains, moisten it with a solution of 1 teaspoon enzyme presoak and 1 cup warm water. Cover with a clean pad that has been dipped in the solution and wrung nearly dry. Let it stand for 30 minutes. Add enough solution to keep the stain warm and barely moist. When no more stain is removed, flush with water and dry.

●*Acrylic Fabric* ●*Modacrylic* ●*Nylon* ●*Olefin* ●*Polyester* ●*Spandex*
Note: Be sure to remove the sugar residue or it will cause a permanent stain. Blot up the excess

liquid and presoak the stain in a solution of 1 quart warm water, ½ teaspoon liquid detergent, and 1 tablespoon vinegar for 15 minutes. Rinse with water and sponge with rubbing alcohol. Launder as soon as possible. If stain remains, presoak stain in a solution of 1 quart warm water and 1 tablespoon enzyme presoak for 30 minutes. Rinse well with water and allow to dry. Launder as soon as possible.

●*Acrylic Plastic* ●*Aluminum* ●*Asphalt* ●*Bamboo* ●*Brass* ●*Bronze* ●*Cane* ●*Ceramic/Tile* ●*Copper* ●*Cork* ●*Enamel* ●*Glass* ●*Gold* ●*Grout* ●*Iron* ●*Ivory* ●*Jade* ●*Linoleum* ●*Paint/Flat* ●*Paint/Gloss* ●*Pewter* ●*Plexiglas* ●*Polyurethane* ●*Stainless Steel* ●*Tin* ●*Vinyl Clothing* ●*Vinyl Tile* ●*Vinyl Wallcovering* ●*Zinc*
Blot up any excess spill. Wipe the surface with a cloth or sponge dipped in warm sudsy water. Rinse well and wipe dry.

●*Alabaster* ●*Marble*
Blot up the excess. Wipe the surface with a cloth dipped in a solution of washing soda or detergent (not soap) and water. Rinse well and wipe dry. If a stain remains, mix a few drops of ammonia with 1 cup 3% hydrogen peroxide. Soak a white blotter with the solution and place it over the stain. Weight it down with a piece of glass or other heavy object. Continue applying the solution until the stain has been bleached out. Rinse well and wipe dry.

●*Bluestone* ●*Brick* ●*Concrete* ●*Flagstone* ●*Granite* ●*Limestone* ●*Masonry Tile* ●*Slate* ●*Terrazzo*
Mix a solution of washing soda or detergent and warm water. Gently brush stain away with cloth

or soft-bristled brush dipped in the solution. Rinse with clear water and allow to dry.

●Burlap ●Silk ●Wool
Note: Be sure to remove the sugar residue or it will cause a permanent stain. Blot up the excess wine. Spray on a fabric spot remover or sponge the stain with water and apply a Wet Spotter and a few drops of white vinegar. Cover with an absorbent pad dampened with Wet Spotter and let it stand as long as any stain is being removed. Change the pad as it picks up the stain. Keep the pad and stain moist with Wet Spotter and vinegar. Flush with water and repeat until no more stain is being lifted. If any stain does remain, sponge with rubbing alcohol and cover with an absorbent pad dampened with alcohol. Let it remain as long as any stain is being lifted. Change the pad as it picks up the stain and keep both the stain and pad moist with alcohol. Flush thoroughly with water. For stubborn or old stains, try moistening the area with a solution of 1 teaspoon liquid laundry detergent safe for silk or wool and 1 cup warm water. Cover with an absorbent pad dipped in the solution and wrung nearly dry. Let it stand for 30 minutes, adding enough solution to keep the area warm and barely moist. When stain is removed, flush thoroughly with water and allow to dry.

●Carpet/Synthetic ●Carpet/Wool
●Foam Rubber
Note: Be sure to remove the sugar residue or it will cause a permanent stain. Blot up what you can with an absorbent pad. Apply a suitable carpet stain remover. Or, flush the stain on area rugs or sponge carpeting with a solution of 1 quart warm water, ½ teaspoon liquid detergent,

and 1 tablespoon white vinegar. Blot with a clean pad and rinse well with water. If the stain remains, sponge it with a solution of 1 quart warm water and 1 tablespoon enzyme presoak. Blot and flush alternately until no more stain is removed. Rinse with clear water and blot up all the excess liquid with an absorbent pad. Weight down another pad with a piece of glass or other heavy object. When no more liquid is absorbed, allow to thoroughly air dry.

•*Cotton* •*Linen*
Blot up the excess, then pretreat with a laundry soil and stain remover and launder. If that is not possible, presoak the stain in a solution of 1 quart warm water and ½ teaspoon liquid detergent and let stand for 15 minutes. Rinse well with water and sponge area with rubbing alcohol. Rinse again with water and allow to dry. If the stain persists, presoak in a solution of warm water and an enzyme presoak according to package directions. Rinse with water and launder as soon as possible.

•*Felt* •*Fur/Natural* •*Fur/Synthetic*
Blot up the excess stain. Mix dishwashing detergent in hot water and swish to make a great volume of suds. Dip a cloth in only the foam and apply. Rinse with a cloth dampened with clear water. Allow to thoroughly air dry.

•*Leather* •*Suede*
Blot up the excess wine. Mix a solution of mild soap in lukewarm water. Swish to create a great volume of suds. Apply only the foam with a sponge. Rinse well with a clean damp cloth and wipe dry. If suede needs a conditioner, apply a

suede cleaner. For leather, condition with saddle soap.

•*Porcelain Dishes* •*Porcelain Fixtures*
Wash the stain with a cloth dipped in warm sudsy water. Rinse well and wipe dry with a soft cloth. To remove any old or set stains in the bottom of dishes, dip a soft damp cloth into a little baking soda and wipe away any remaining residue. Rinse well and wipe dry.

•*Silver*
Wash silver in hot soapy water. Rinse in hot water and wipe dry with a soft cloth.

•*Wood*
Mix dishwashing detergent in hot water and swish to make a great volume of suds. Dip a cloth in only the foam and apply to the stain. Rinse well with a clean cloth dampened with cool water. Polish or wax as soon as possible.

Wine/White

(*Follow procedures for* Alcoholic Beverages.)

Yellowing

•*Acetate* •*Fiberglass* •*Rayon* •*Silk* •*Triacetate* •*Wool*
Flush the spot with water. Test a mild solution

of 3% hydrogen peroxide and water in an inconspicuous area—if safe, apply gingerly to the stain. Do not allow the solution to remain on the fabric; flush with water immediately. If any stain remains, it is best not to attempt further cleaning at home.

●Acrylic Fabric ●Modacrylic ●Nylon ●Olefin ●Polyester

Apply lemon juice to the stain, but do not let it dry. Rinse thoroughly with water. If possible, launder. If you can't launder, test a suitable rust remover on an inconspicuous area. If safe to use, apply according to package directions. Then flush the area with cool water and launder as soon as possible. Be careful not to spill any rust remover on porcelain or enamel, as it will ruin the finish.

●Cotton ●Linen

Rub detergent into the stain and rinse well with water. Launder as soon as possible. If the stain remains, test a rust remover in an inconspicuous place. If safe, apply according to package directions. Flush thoroughly with water and launder.

●Linoleum ●Vinyl Tile

Wipe the stain with a cloth or sponge dipped in warm sudsy water to which a few drops of ammonia have been added. Rinse with a cloth moistened with clear water and wipe dry.

●Porcelain Dishes ●Porcelain Fixtures

Make a paste of borax and lemon juice. Rub it into the stain and allow to dry. Rinse with clear water and repeat if necessary. Rinse thoroughly and dry with a soft cloth.

TRADEMARKS OF SYNTHETIC FIBERS

Trademark	Generic Name
A	
A.C.E.	nylon or polyester
Acetate by Avtex	acetate
Absorbit	rayon
Acrilan	acrylic or modacrylic
Anso	nylon
Antron	nylon
Ariloft	acetate
Arnel	triacetate
Avlin	polyester
Avril	rayon
Avron	acetate
Avsorb	rayon
B	
Beau-Grip	rayon
Bi-Loft	acrylic
Blue "C"	nylon or polyester
C	
Cadon	nylon
Cantrece	nylon
Caprolan	nylon or polyester
Captiva	nylon
Celanese	nylon or acetate
Chromspun	acetate
Coloray	rayon
Cordura	nylon
Courcel	rayon
Courtaulds HT Rayon	rayon
Courtaulds Nylon	nylon
Courtaulds Rayon	rayon

Crepesoft	polyester
Creslan	acrylic
Cumuloft	nylon

D

Dacron	polyester
Durvil	rayon

E

Eloquent Luster	nylon
Eloquent Touch	nylon
Encron	polyester
Enkacrepe	nylon
Enkaire	rayon
Enkalon	nylon
Enkalure	nylon
Enkasheer	nylon
Enkrome	rayon
Estron	acetate

F

Fibro	rayon
Fi-lana	acrylic
Fortrel	polyester

G

Golden Glow	polyester
Golden Touch	polyester

H

Herculon	olefin
Herculon Nouvelle	olefin
Hollofil	polyester

K

Kevlar	aramid
Kodaire	polyester

Kodel	polyester
KodOfill	polyester
KodOlite	polyester
KodOsoff	polyester

L

Lethasuede	polyester
Loftura	acetate
Lurelon	nylon
Lusterloff	nylon
Lycra	spandex

M

Marquesa Lana	olefin
Marvess	olefin
Matte Touch	polyester
Multisheer	nylon

N

Natural Luster	nylon
Natural Touch	nylon or polyester
Nomex	aramid
No Shock	nylon

O

| Orlon | acrylic |

P

Pa-Qel	acrylic
Patlon	olefin
Plyloc	polyester
Polyextra	polyester

R

| Rayon by Avtex | rayon |
| Remember | acrylic |

S
SEF	modacrylic
Shanton	polyester
Shareen	nylon
Shimmereen	nylon
Silky Touch	polyester
Softalon	nylon
So-Lara	acrylic
Strialine	polyester

T
T.E.N.	nylon
Trevira	polyester

U
Ultraglow	polyester
Ultra Touch	polyester
Ultron	nylon

V
Vinyon by Avtex	vinyon

Z
Zantrel	rayon
Zefkrome	acrylic
Zefran	acrylic or nylon
Zeftron	nylon

The basic fiber trademarks listed are registered by the member companies of the Man-Made Fiber Producers Association that are currently active. The list does not include service marks, guarantees, warranties or variations of the basic fiber trademark.

Reprinted with permission of the Man-Made Fiber Producers Association, Inc.